China's Museums | Cultural China Series

China's
Museums

Li Xianyao
Luo Zhewen

Translated by Martha Avery

CHINA
INTERCONTINENTAL
PRESS

图书在版编目（CIP）数据

中国博物馆／黎先耀，罗哲文编著；罗哲文等摄；(美)艾梅霞(Avery, M.)译.—北京：五洲传播出版社，2004.10
ISBN 7-5085-0603-0

Ⅰ.中... Ⅱ.①黎...②罗...③罗...④艾... Ⅲ.博物馆—简介—中国—英文 Ⅳ.G269.26

中国版本图书馆 CIP 数据核字（2004）第 105171 号

中国博物馆

编 著 者／黎先耀、罗哲文

摄 影 者／罗哲文、黎先耀、梁秀云、杨静云等

译 者／(美)艾梅霞(Martha Avery)

责任编辑／邓锦辉

整体设计／海 洋

出版发行／五洲传播出版社 （北京海淀区莲花池东路北小马场6号 邮编:100038)

版式制作／张 红

承 印 者／北京华联印刷有限公司

开 本／720×965毫米 1/16

字 数／120千字

印 张／13.25

版 次／2004年10月第1版

印 次／2004年10月第1次印刷

书 号／ISBN 7-5085-0603-0/G·97

定 价／96.00元

Table of Contents

Foreword:
Reading the History of Chinese Civilization from Its Museums

China has an ancient civilization with a very long history. Understanding it solely through the study of documents is clearly inadequate. A wealth of objects and remains has been preserved on China's vast territory and underground; much of which has been collected and is exhibited in various kinds of museums. This raw material of history can, in a certain sense, be considered more valuable for our understanding of the past than documents and historical records.

One can see many of China's cultural treasures in Western museums. Some of these are exquisite works of art, but at the same time they are fragments that have been removed from the original matrix of their being. To enjoy a complete and systematic experience of Chinese cultural history, one must visit the museums of their native land. Although there are Dunhuang sutras in the British Museum, stolen by Aurel Stein, Dunhuang itself and the center of Dunhuang Studies remain in China. Although quite a few treasures from the Summer Palace were looted by British and French troops and are now exhibited in France at Fontainebleu, the majority of choice pieces remains in the Palace Museum in Beijing.

In the past, China's antiquities and most artworks were kept in the recesses of the residences of aristocratic families

and the imperial clan. The public at large was not able to see them. China's modern museums started from the Westernization Movement of the early twentieth century and the overthrow of the feudal imperial court during the Xinhai Revolution (1911). Only after this was the public allowed to enter the halls and pavilions and enjoy the fruits of the civilization of their own ancestors. In the past twenty to thirty years, due to China's opening and reform policy as well as to the development of a market economy, travel, tourism, and cultural exchange have greatly increased. China's socialist museums have developed along with these changes: they have been rebuilding and expanding old museums, adding new buildings, increasing collections, modernizing exhibition facilities and strengthening archaeological research. There are now some 2,000 museums in China of all varieties. Visitors from both China and abroad have increased, with very positive results in the realm of education as well as in simple enjoyment.

Museums are a sort of three-dimensional encyclopedia. In the West, the Goddess of the Muse has been considered a kind of guide to Western culture. The Temple of the Muse at Atlantis was originally a comprehensive cultural arts

organization and Western museums harken back to this early beginning. In China, museums originated in the collections of the ancient imperial families. They too were of a comprehensive nature and the cultural guide to the East was termed a '*bo-wu*' gentleman, or a man in command of broad or extensive matters. The term 'museum' in China, '*bo-wu-guan,*' means a place devoted to broadly-conceived matters.

Many of the museums selected for this book have been designated as key protected cultural sites by China. Some have been included in the United Nations' UNESCO List of World Cultural Heritage Sites. I hope that this volume can serve visitors as a guide to understanding these museums.

Li Xianyao
October 2003, Beijing

National Treasures

China is an ancient country with tremendous creative capacity. Its museums are a treasure trove of Eastern civilization. If you are able to place yourself in their midst, you will find that they delight the eye and nourish the mind.

6

Palace Museum

◆ Address: Beijing, Jingshan Front Street, #4 (Jingshan Qian Jie, #4)
◆ Website: http://www.dpm.org.cn

The Palace Museum is situated in the center of Beijing, the capital city of China. It was established on October 10, 1925, and is China's largest museum.

The museum is also known as the 'Purple' Forbidden City in Chinese, or the Forbidden City as it is commonly known in English. It covers 720,000 square meters and was the imperial palace for a succession of twenty-four emperors and their dynasties during the Ming and Qing periods of Chinese history. The museum is also China's largest and most complete architectural grouping of ancient halls. Construction was begun in 1420, the eighteenth year of Yongle, so that the site has

The Palace Museum.

The Three Great Halls in the Forbidden City.

existed for the past 580 years.

More than 70 halls of various sizes, containing more than 9,000 rooms, comprise the Forbidden City. These halls are aligned along a north-south axis, and extend out on either side in an east-west symmetry. The central axis not only passes through the Purple Forbidden City, but extends south to Yongding Gate and north to the Bell and Drum Towers, for a length of some eight kilometers. This passage through the entire city of Beijing symbolizes the centrality of the imperial power: the imperial seat is at the very center of this line. The architectural design lines up the buildings in neat array and with imposing scale. In a concentrated form, this assemblage expresses China's artistic traditions in the setting of China's unique architectural style.

Entering the Forbidden City from Tian'an Men, one first moves straight through the Duan Gate to arrive at Wu Men, or the great Wu Gate. The popular name for Wu Men is the Five Phoenix Tower; this is the front entrance to the Purple Forbidden City. Going through Wu Men, spread out before one is a broad courtyard with the twisting course of the Jinshui Creek (Gold Water Creek) passing from west to east like a jade belt. Five marble bridges have been constructed over this waterway. Passing through the Taihe Gate to the north of the bridges

The recessed ceiling of the Taihe Hall in the Forbidden City.

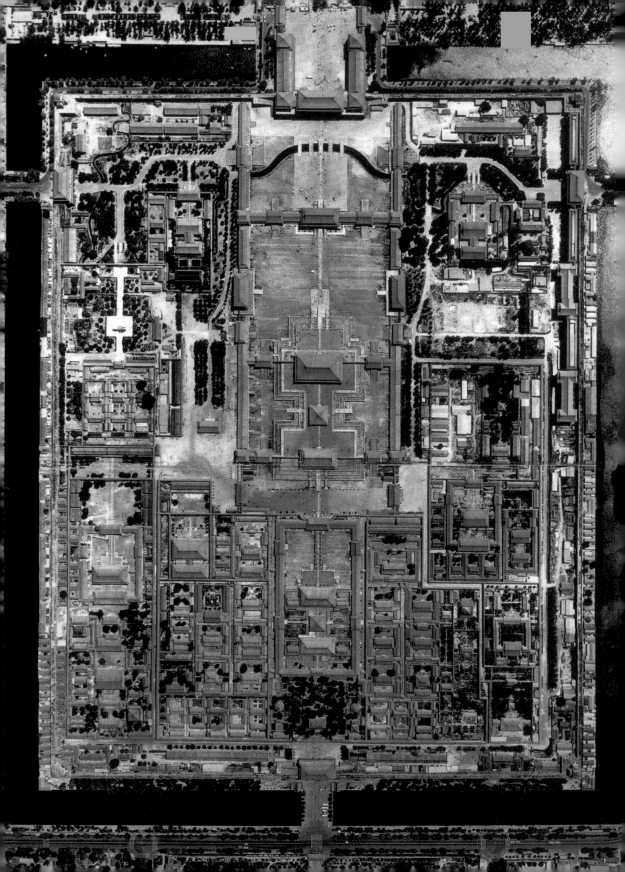

one reaches the core of the Purple Forbidden City, the famous three great halls called Taihe Hall, Zhonghe Hall, and Baohe Hall.

Taihe Hall is 28 meters high and occupies a space of around 2,380 square meters. It is the largest hall in the Palace. A red-lacquered dais around two meters high sits in its center, on which is placed a golden lacquered and carved dragon throne. Behind the throne is a screen carved with dragons and on either side of the dais are six great golden pillars with vigorous golden dragons coiling up them. In the recessed ceiling well above the throne is an extremely large coiled golden dragon, with a silvery pearl suspended from its mouth. The Taihe Hall was the location of the Emperor's most important ceremonies, such as his own inauguration, his birthday, New Years, the arrival of winter, and so on.

Behind the Taihe Hall lies the Zhonghe Hall. This is a square hall with four ridge poles along the roofline that unite at the top in a large, round, gilded topknot called a *baoding*. The profile of the building is extremely beautiful. When the Emperor was about to officiate at important ceremonies, he would first rest in this building and receive visits of his various Ministers.

Behind the Zhonghe Hall is the Baohe Hall. In the Qing dynasty, every New Year's Eve, the Emperor would hold a great banquet in this hall. This also was where the highest exam of the *Ke-ju* exam system was held.

Emerging from the Baohe Hall and following the stone stairs downwards one arrives at an open rectangular courtyard. This space divides the Purple Forbidden City into front and back. To the south of the square are the three main Halls and, to east and west of them are the Wenhua Hall and the Wuying Hall. These are commonly called the 'Outer Court,' where the Emperor primarily conducted affairs of state. To the north of the square, inside the Qianqing Gate, was the Inner Sanctum. In the

The marble royal ramp of the Baohe Hall in the Forbidden City.

10

The bridal chamber for emperors of the Qing dynasty.

Qing dynasty, this is where the Emperor and his Empresses and Concubines lived. The main buildings include the Qianqing Palace, the Jiaotai Hall, the Kunning Palace, and six palaces to east and west.

The Qianqing Palace was at one time where the Emperor slept. During the Qing dynasty, however, the emperors used this as a place of daily administrative affairs. Later emperors also met foreign emissaries here. Behind the Qianqing Palace is the Jiaotai Hall, which is where memorials to the Empress were conducted and where she received congratulations on her birthday. It also is where the Qing dynasty's twenty-five 'treasures' were kept, the twenty-five seals by use of which the Emperor manifested his rule. Behind the Jiaotai Hall is the Kunning Palace, which was originally a sleeping chamber for the Empress. Later in the Qing dynasty it was made into a place where offerings to gods were made and also where the Emperor was married.

The Thousand Autumn Pavilion in the Imperial Garden in the Forbidden City.

The Qianqing Palace, the Jiaotai Hall, and the Kunning Palace together constituted the Rear Three Palaces, their placement being basically the same as the Front Three Halls, but with decoration and coloring that were markedly different. The Front Three Halls used dragons as a primary motif. The Rear Three Palaces saw phoenixes gradually increase until there were numerous flying phoenixes, dancing phoenixes, phoenixes with peonies and other such decorative elements.

The East and West Six Palaces, where the concubines lived, were commonly known as the 'Three Palaces and Six Courtyards.' Today the Six Palaces of the East have been made into exhibition halls in order to display the rare paintings, ceramics, bronzes, and various crafts that were collected and kept in the Palace. The Six Palaces of the West are basically as they were, unchanged, so that people can see the actual living conditions of the feudal period, the historical reality of how royalty lived.

The most notable building is the Yangxin Hall, the Cultivating the Mind Hall. Qing-dynasty emperors mostly lived here, from the Emperor Yongzheng onward, or for some two hundred years. The Yangxin Hall therefore became the center of daily governing activities. Emperors often received

The dragon throne in the Taihe Hall in the Forbidden City.

Ministers here and issued decrees and orders. Two thrones were placed in the eastern room of the Yangxin Hall, to front and back; between them was suspended a golden-colored screen. This was where the Empress Dowager Cixi ruled from behind the screen (she lived from 1835-1908, was of the clan of Yehenala, and she ruled from behind the screen in two periods in 1861 and 1873).

From the Yangxin Hall moving northwards, one courtyard succeeds another in quiet elegance and serenity. Among these are the Changquan Palace and the Zhuxiu Palace, the latter being where Cixi once lived. Right now, the display in the Zhuxiu Palace is as Cixi had it arranged on the occasion of her fiftieth birthday.

Emerging from the Zhuxiu Palace, not far to the east, is the Yuhua Garden, or Imperial Garden. The area of the Yuhua Garden is small and intimate; its architecture and atmosphere are completely different from the front parts of the Palace. The pavilions and small buildings are set in the midst of pools and pine trees, fake mountains appear to be made of grotesque stones, there are potted garden landscapes, wisteria and bamboo. In the northeast of the Palace is also the

The Taihe Hall in the Forbidden City.

Ningshou Palace Garden, where the Emperor Qianlong (Qing dynasty Gaozong Aisin-Gioro Hongli 1736-1795) cultivated his mind after returning to power.

13

Coming out of the Yuhua Garden and following the passageway, one arrives at the northern gate of the Purple Forbidden City called the Shenwu Men. Opposite this gate is Jingshan Mountain. This small hill was built from dirt that came from digging out the moat when the Ming dynasty was building the Purple Forbidden City. Standing on the top of the hill and looking out over the Palace one sees wave after wave of buildings, crest after crest of rooflines and walls.

The Purple Forbidden City is also a great treasury of art objects. Great collections of paintings, calligraphy, sculpture, inscriptions, bronzes, ceramics, textiles and embroideries, jewels, clocks, articles made of gold and silver, and so on are kept here. The collection contains around 900,000 items. The Palace Museum also has preserved around nine million historical documents and materials from the Ming and Qing dynasties. These represent an important original resource for the study of the past five hundred years of China's history. Many of the more important documents can be seen in the special exhibition hall of the Palace.

The Sanxi Hall (Three Treasure Hall) in the Palace Museum that collects ancient calligraphic treasures.

Hall of 'Art through the Dynasties'

This is located in the Baohe Hall and in subsidiary buildings to its east and west. Treasures are exhibited here that range from Early Society to the Qing dynasty. Altogether around 6,000 years of history are displayed through 1,600 articles. Each of the displayed objects is a work of art and can be considered a treasure selected from amongst treasures. This hall has three rooms: the first is in Baohe Hall and exhibits pieces from the late period of Early Society to the Spring and Autumn period; the second room displays items from the Warring States period to the Song dynasty; the third room displays art objects of the Yuan, Ming, and Qing dynasties.

Qing Dynasty Display Room of 'Decrees and Regulations' and Cultural Artifacts

This is located in the eastern corridor of the Qianqing Palace. The items displayed here were used by the Qing-dynasty emperors to carry out affairs of state, the hold ceremonies and rituals, and to go hunting. Exhibited here are four main different kinds of objects: personal treasures of the Emperor, musical instruments of the court, clothes of the Empress, and weapons and arms.

Qing Palace Exhibition Hall of Toys

This exhibition displays toys that were mostly made in the eighteenth and ninetheenth centuries and given to the Qing court by Switzerland, France, England, and Germany. Also exhibited are some items made by the Qing Palace Workshops and some made by the people of Guangdong. The toys can be divided into two types, mechanized and general toys. The mechanized category includes objects that have an internal mechanism that makes them move: birds call out, animals move, and so on. Some of the general toys were actually used by children; some were given to the court to be used as decoration in the halls.

Hall of Bronzes

This is located in two palaces called the Zhai Palace and the Jingren Palace. Some 400 pieces are exhibited that range from the Shang and Zhou periods to the Warring States period. In the Shang and Zhou slave society, bronzes were regarded as ceremonial objects that differentiated one's status. By the Warring States period, items appeared that were actually used by the then appearing feudal system such as coins, stamps or seals, tallies, measuring devices and so on.

Hall of Ceramics

This is in the two palaces called the Chengqian Palace and the Yonghe Palace, and contains four rooms that exhibit around 700 objects. China is the homeland of ceramics. 'Painted pottery' already existed some 6,000 years ago here; by the time of the Shang dynasty, primitive porcelains were being fired; after another 1,000 years, actual porcelain was made during the Eastern Han period.

Four Treasures of the Scholar's Studio

Zhongcui Palace was one of the halls in Six Palaces of the East, but now it has been designated as the Hall of the Four Treasures of the Scholar's Studio. These include brushes, ink, paper, and inkstands, each of which has its aesthetics and connoisseurship. For example, the manufacture of ink and inkstands can require of the maker a high degree of technical as well as aesthetic skill. Because of this, great value is placed on fine inks and inkstands in China. The paper and inkstands, brushes and ink that are exhibited here come from many dynasties. Displayed here are the famous 'Hu Brush,' 'Hui Ink,' 'Xuanzhi or Xuan paper,' and 'Duan inkstands.'

Ming-Qing Minor Arts and Crafts Gallery

A wealth of Ming- and Qing-dynasty crafts items collected by the Palace is exhibited in the Jingyang Palace. The diversity of items here includes lacquer objects, jade objects, glass objects, enamel objects, gold and other metallic objects, as well as bamboo, wood, and carved ivory.

The Clock Gallery

Fengxian Hall is where the Qing-dynasty emperors made offerings to the tablets of their ancestors; now it has been opened up and made into the Clock Gallery. These clocks were mainly collected during the Qianlong and Jiaqing periods of the Qing dynasty (1736-1820). Some were made in Guangzhou and Suzhou, as well as the workshop within the Palace, others came from England, France, and Switzerland. Clocks made in China were mostly decorated with gold, pearls, jade, and gems. Their form reflected traditional architectural forms such as pagodas, towers, and miniature landscapes. The clocks of England, France and other countries in turn imitated Western styles and architecture.

Hall of Paintings

This is located in Huangji Hall and the Ningshou Palace. Around 100,000 paintings are kept here that range in date from the Jin to the Qing dynasty and that include paintings and calligraphy of many famous masters. October in Beijing has fresh air with a suitable temperature and low humidity. As a result, works of the Jin, Tang, Song, and Yuan dynasties are generally exhibited every year at this time. Some of the world-famous treasures that are exhibited include ones by Lu Ji (261-303, Jin dynasty), Yan Liben (601-673, Tang dynasty), Gu Hongzhong (Five Dynasties Southern Tang painter), Zhang Zeduan (uncertain dates of birth and death, famous Song-dynasty painter), and so on, as well as Yan Zhenqing (709-785, Tang-dynasty calligrapher), Liu Gongquan (778-865, Tang-dynasty calligrapher), Mi Fu (1051-1107, Northern Song painter and calligrapher), and so on. Ming- and Qing-dynasty painters are also exhibited at certain times in the year.

Inscriptions Hall

Inscriptions, rubbings, and seals from various dynasties are displayed in the Inscriptions Gallery of the Huangji Hall.

Han Xizai's Evening Banquet *painted by Gu Hongzhong.*   The Yangxin Hall in the Forbidden City.

Treasures Gallery

These are displayed in three halls that were formerly for other purposes but were opened up to form this exhibition. On display here are gold and silver, jade and exotic items collected by the Qing court. These were all used for various purposes including ceremonial, sacrificial, as clothing, as ornament, and in daily life, as well as to adorn the rooms of the court.

Taipei Palace Museum

◆ Address: Taiwan, Taipei City, Shilin Wai Shuangxi Zhishan Lu Er Duan, #221
◆ Website: http://www.npm.gov.tw

The Taipei Palace Museum is located in the northwestern part of Taipei City, facing Shuangxi Park and surrounded by verdant trees and rolling hills. The palace was constructed as a replica of the Beijing Palace Museum. It has an area of more than 10,000 square meters and is grand and imposing in character. Approximately some 620,000 historical items and works of art are stored here, in a magnificent four-storied building. The construction of the Taipei Palace Museum was begun in 1962 and completed in the summer of 1965. Some 240,000 of the items that are kept here originally belonged to the Beijing Palace Museum.

In 1949, 3,824 crates of objects were moved to Taiwan. Among these were the

A panorama of the Taipei Palace Museum.

The Taipei Palace Museum.

Mao Gong ding *(a kind of ancient vessel).*

great treasures of 'hua-xia,' a term that also means China, but in a more comprehensive cultural sense, including Shang and Zhou bronzes, jades, works of calligraphy from Jin and Tang dynasties onward, paintings from Tang and Song dynasties onward, ceramics from famous kilns from Song and Yuan dynasties onward, bamboo items, rare books, documents from the Qing dynasty, as well as sculptures, jades, lacquer works, enamels, and so on.

Most of the items on display are shown in the main building of the museum. This building is divided into four levels, with the main entrance being on the second floor. The great hall of the second floor has a bronze bust of Sun Zhongshan (Sun Yatsen), made as a replica of the one in Nanjing at Sun Yatsen's tomb. All around this sculpture hang very famous paintings and works of calligraphy; in the corridor leading to Sun Yatsen are two of the most famous long scrolls in the history of Chinese art.

Several national treasures are on the must-see list for visitors. Among these is the Mao Gong *ding* dating from

The Sanxi Hall Tea House in the Taipei Palace Museum.

Western Zhou, unearthed during the latter years of the Qing dynasty in the Daoguang reign (1850) in the province of Shaanxi. The height of this *ding* is 53.8 centimeters and its diameter is 47.9 centimeters. It has three legs or feet and two upright handles or ears. Its ornamentation is very simple as is the exterior. On the inside of the *Ding* is an inscription of 491 characters – the longest inscription of any known Chinese bronze.

A large number of calligraphies and paintings by famous painters are exhibited in the Taipei Palace Museum. These include Li Gonglin (1049-1106, notable Song-dynasty painter), Chen Juzhong (years of birth and death unclear, a Southern-Song painter), Qiu Ying (around 1509-1551, a Ming-dynasty painter), Wang Hui (1632-1717, an early Qing-dynasty painter), Fan Kuan (around 950-1027, Song-dynasty painter), Guo Xi (1023-around 1085, Song-dynasty painter), Wang Xizhi (303-361) and so on.

The Taipei Palace Museum also contains a number of famous items of the scholar's studio. Among these the

The jade Chinese cabbage displayed in the Taipei Palace Museum.

20

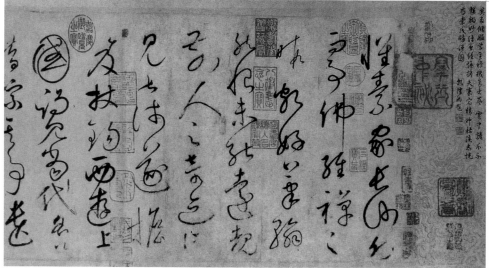

Huai Su's calligraphy displayed in the Taipei Palace Museum.

most representative is the inkstone of the Song-dynasty Su Dongpo (1037-1101), the northern Song calligrapher and literati figure, also the inkstone of Zhao Mengfu (1254-1322), the famous Yuan-dynasty calligrapher.

The permanent display of the Taipei Palace Museum contains twenty thousand objects. These are rotated once every three months. Every ten years is a full cycle, so that even rare objects can be exhibited and seen by everyone.

Shanghai Museum

◆ Address: Shanghai, Peoples Great Road, #201
◆ Website: http://www.shanghaimuseum.net

The scope, depth and quality of its collections, and the striking architecture and use of modern technology make the Shanghai Museum one of the most famous if not the most famous in China. It covers an area of 38,000 square meters, with a scale that surpasses the old museum severalfold. The exterior of the museum utilizes the shape of an ancient bronze ding, specifically a Chen *ding*, with its rather archaic flavor. The structure and materials of the entire building, however, are an accomplishment of the most modern technology.

The Shanghai Museum.

A wood carving Guanyin statue of the Song dynasty.

The stairs and the skylight of the Shanghai Museum.

The Shanghai Museum is mainly a museum for ancient arts. At present it is divided into ten sections. These are: ancient Chinese bronzes, sculpture, ceramics, jades, seals, calligraphy, coin and currency, paintings, Ming and Qing-dynasty furniture, and crafts of China's national minorities. In addition to these ten permanent exhibitions, the museum often holds small-scale exhibitions and also exhibits articles from elsewhere on a short-term basis. The Museum also exhibits its material in museums both within China and abroad.

Among the holdings of the Museum many items are superlative works of art and are unique in the entire country. These include in particular the bronzes, calligraphy, paintings, and Ming and Qing furniture.

China's Shang and Zhou-period bronzes are an important testimony to the ancient civilization of the country. When visitors enter the Ancient Bronzes Hall, the presentation and atmosphere of the rooms expresses the cultural atmosphere of the bronze age. The subdued dark-green tone of the walls imparts an ancient atmosphere, the simple and elegant display cases and the lighting are carefully designed to enhance the experience. Some 400 exquisite bronze items are displayed in a space of 1,200 square meters, perfectly reflecting the history of the development of China's ancient bronze arts.

The Calligraphy Hall includes works from many dynasties; in chronological order it displays the history of the marvelous genius of Chinese calligraphic arts. The aura of the hall is scholarly and elegant, assisted by automatic lighting in display cases that protects the art by shining only when the visitor is viewing a work. Among these works are a number of unique world treasures.

The Chinese Painting Hall of the Museum similarly has a touch of traditional architectural style to it, combined with an atmosphere of Confucian elegance.

Furnitures of the Ming and Qing dynasties displayed in the Shanghai Museum.

Around 120 masterpieces are displayed in the 1,200-square-meter exhibition space. These date from the Tang dynasty to modern times but do not include contemporary works.

The apex of Chinese furniture creation occurred during the Ming and Qing dynasties. Walking into the Ming and Qing Furniture Hall is like walking back into the gardens and rooms of the Ming and Qing dynasty. In some 700 square meters of space are exhibited some 100 pieces of superlative Chinese Ming and Qing-dynasty furniture. Among these are Ming pieces that are fluid in line and harmonious in proportion. The Qing pieces have more complex ornamentation and are often made of thicker, heavier wood.

The underground part of the Shanghai Museum also has some courtyard gardens that imitate authentic Chinese traditions. Although these are hidden deeply underground, their architecture and environment seem light and airy.

Da Ke ding (a kind of ancient vessel).

24

Shaanxi History Museum

◆ Address: Shaanxi Province, Xi'an City, Yanta Road, #70
◆ Webpage: http://www.sxhm.com

The Shaanxi History Museum is situated on Yan Ta Road in Xi'an City, Shaanxi Province. It covers 65,000 square meters, with a building area of 60,000 square meters. The newly built modern building recreates Tang-dynasty architecture and successfully symbolizes the great extent of Shaanxi history and its remarkable culture.

Exhibited in the main exhibition hall are 2,700 works of art, with an exhibition line that extends 2,300 meters. The exhibition space is divided into an introductory hall, permanent exhibitions, special exhibitions, and temporary exhibitions, as

The exterior of the Shaanxi History Museum.

An exhibition of tomb frescoes of the Tang dynasty.

A cup-holding leather bag style silver kettle of the Tang dynasty with gold-plating horses unearthed in Xi'an.

A Tang-dynasty gold bowl with lotus petals carving unearthed in Xi'an.

well as one that has been named the National Painting Hall.

The Museum's permanent exhibition primarily displays Shaanxi's ancient history. Representative pieces from all periods have been selected to show the development of civilization in this region. The exhibition space of this display is 4,600 square meters. It includes three exhibition rooms, divided into seven parts (Prehistory, Zhou, Qin, Han, Wei-Jin-North and South dynasties, Sui-Tang, and Song-Yuan-Ming-Qing). The superlative 2,000 selected objects include: painted Neolithic ceramics reflecting early people's living conditions and their pursuit of vibrant art forms, bronzes reflecting the rise of Zhou people, bronze weapons including swords, and statuary of horses and soldiers, reflecting the way in which Qin unified all under heaven, Tang-dynasty gold and silver objects and Tang sancai ceramics, reflecting the most flourishing period of feudal glory. All of this is accompanied by models of archaeological sites, and drawings, and photographs. These works systematically exhibit the ancient history of Shaanxi from 150,000 years ago to the year 1840. Since several historical periods all based their capitals on

26

A Tang-triple-color ceramic camel that carries a small musical band on its back with a female performer standing in the middle singing and dancing.

Shaanxi territory, such as Zhou, Qin, Western Han, Sui and Tang, the exhibits emphasize these periods and these places. This not only expresses the extent of culture in ancient Shaanxi, it also displays the highest level of cultural development of China's social economy.

The temporary exhibits hall, located on the east side of the museum, has had a variety of exhibitions including Tang-tomb wall paintings, that is to say 39 of the actual paintings. Shaanxi's wall murals of this kind rank first in the entire country. They are fluid in concept and line, they have marvelous details, and they both depict Tang customs and are superb works of art.

The special exhibition hall is located on the west side of the museum. Its first two exhibitions were a Shaanxi bronzes exhibit (260 were on display) and a Shaanxi-through-the-dynasties terracotta masterpieces exhibit (341 objects were exhibited). The area of this hall is around 2,600 square meters.

The Shaanxi History Museum contains 115,000 objects in its collections. The more representative of these include bronzes, Tang-dynasty tomb wall paintings, terracotta statuary, ceramics (pottery and porcelain), construction materials through the dynasties, Han and Tang bronze mirrors, and coins and currency, calligraphy, rubbings, scrolls, woven articles, bone articles, wooden and lacquer and iron and stone objects, seals, as well as some contemporary cultural relics and ethnic objects.

A bronze ox zun *(a kind of ancient wine vessel) of the Western Zhou Dynasty unearthed in Qishan County, Shaanxi Province.*

Henan Museum

◆ Address: Henan Province, Zhengzhou City, Nongye Road, #8
◆ Webpage: http://www.chnmus.net

The Henan Museum is one of China's oldest museums. It is a 'key' museum, with modern displays and exhibitions, modernized equipment, and a unique architecture. In 1961, along with the move of the provincial capital to Zhengzhou, it moved to its current location. In 1991 that museum was remodeled and in 1999 the official reopening was held, when the name was officially declared the Henan Museum.

The facade of the Henan Museum.

The new Henan Museum is set in the central section of Nongye Road in Zhengzhou City, Henan Province. It covers an area of more than 100,000 square meters, with a building area of 78,000 square meters. The exhibition hall space is more than 10,000 square meters. The building uses a combination of both traditional architecture and pathbreaking new technology.

Henan is situated in the middle reaches of the Yellow River. Its ancient name is Zhongzhou, or central region. It is one of the important areas for the rise of the Chinese people's early civilization. Because of this, exhibitions in this museum are mostly related to the ancient history and culture of the Henan region, including objects, historical traces, ancient architecture, archaeological discoveries and arts and crafts.

In the past several decades, the collecting, protection, research, and exhibition of this museum's artifacts as well as their promotion and educational material on them have seen great advances. Objects from the Museum's collections have

A rose-purple Chinese flowering crabapple style ceramic flower pot unearthed in Yu County, Henan Province.

A Warring States period gold-plating silver belt hook inlaid with jade unearthed in Hui County, Henan Province.

The representative display in the main hall of the Henan Museum.

traveled to America, Japan, England, Germany, France, Australia, and Denmark for exhibition and have been widely praised. The Henan Museum applies modern management systems, its security systems of surveillance and alarms are consolidated into a central unit, to ensure the safety of the objects. The automatic management system of the buildings can monitor and adjust all of the surveillance and condition systems of the various buildings. This enables ambient environmental conditions to be monitored and adjusted, to protect the collections and exhibited objects and to control the required levels of temperature and humidity.

< *An article for the dead of Han dynasty displayed in the Henan Museum (architectural model).*

32

Nanjing Museum

◆ Address: Jiangsu Province, Nanjing City, Zhongshan East Road, #321
◆ Webpage: http://www.njmuseum.com

The Nanjing Museum is located inside the Zhongshan Gate of Nanjing City. Its predecessor was known as the Central Museum Preparatory Location. The complex of buildings represents an amalgamation of east and west, with the great hall copying the style of a Liao-dynasty palace.

The Museum currently holds some 400,000 objects in its collections, among

*The facade of the main building
of the Nanjing Museum.*

The outdoor courtyard layout of the Nanjing Museum.

which are some of the most famous objects in China. These include the only complete set of 'jade suits sewed with silver thread' in China, which are world renowned. In 1982, a Warring States period Chu State tomb was excavated from which stellar pieces were retrieved that also form some of the extraordinary treasures in this museum.

The calligraphy and paintings collections are also very special. Among the 100,000 objects that have officially entered the collections, most are Ming- and Qing-dynasty works of artists who lived in the Jiangsu area. Among these, the most special are the 'Wu Men painting school,' 'Yangzhou painting school,' Jinling painting school,' as well as a small number of Song and Yuan-dynasty works. Most of the representative works of the modern Chinese painter

A south-of-Yangtze family's living room displayed in the Nanjing Museum.

An Eastern Han dynasty copper ox lamp inlaid with silver.

A Warring States period copper kettle inlaid with gold beasts.

Fu Baoshi (1904-1965, painter, art historian), and Chen Zhifo (1896-1962, modern arts educator) are stored here.

The Nanjing Museum holds the objects excavated by archaeologists in the early part of the twentieth century that were moved to Nanjing when the Palace Museum moved southward. These include excavations in Heilongjiang, Xinjiang, Yunnan, Sichuan, Gansu and other places. Collections also include artifacts from the southwest parts of China of the Naxi tribe, the Yi tribe, the Miao tribe, and other national minorities.

The Museum applies modern scientific methods of conservation, and is active in displaying its holdings, having mounted some 236 exhibitions.

Liaoning Provincial Museum

◆ Address: Liaoning Province, Shenyang City, Heping District, Shiwei Road, #26
◆ Website: http://www.zgjt.com/CARSHOW/bowuguan.html

The exterior of the Liaoning Provincial Museum.

The Liaoning Provincial Museum is located in Heping District of Shenyang City, Liaoning Province. The area of the Museum grounds and buildings totals 110,000 square meters. The heart of the Museum is a three-story exhibition hall that was designed by a German architect. In 1988, a new three-story white building was built inside the grounds that includes a large hall and a surrounding corridor.

Historical artifacts and ancient arts are the main focus of the Museum's collections. These include some eighteen categories of objects: paintings and calligraphy, embroideries, woodblock prints, bronzes, ceramics, lacquerware, carvings, oracle bones, celadons, costumes, archaeological material, coins and currency, stelaes, old maps, ethnic minority artifacts, revolutionary artifacts, furniture, and assorted other items. Among these some were excavated and others were passed down through the ages, that is inherited, not recovered from the earth. The collections occupy an important position among museums' collections in China.

Painting and calligraphy collections include paintings by famous Tang-dynasty and Northern Song artists, and woodblock-print editions include the Ming-dynasty Album of the Ten-bamboo Studio, the first colored woodblock print in Chinese woodblock-print history.

The ceramics collections in the museum are also quite famous and valuable. Liao porcelain is unique in the art form for its treatment of colored glazes, but the collection also includes Liao monochromes such as the lovely Liao white porcelain. Many of the ceramic forms embody nomadic characteristics, and the glazes and colors are imbued with local character. Production methods continue the traditions of the Tang and Five dynasties kilns.

Two permanent collections are on display in the museum. One is an exhibit on Chinese history, and the other is a display of stone inscriptions. The former deals with overall Chinese history in general but also takes local Liao history into special consideration. Contents include:

Room 1: The main archaeological findings from Paleolithic and Neolithic times in the Liaoning region. Key emphases are on the sites from early Paleolithic times at Yingkou Jinniu Shan, the Paleolithic cave site at Hezi Cave, the Hongshan Culture site, the Shenyang Xinle early Neolithic site, the Lushun Guojia Cun site, and so on.

Room 2: Key exhibits include a Xiajiadian Lower-level-culture site that corresponds to Xia and Shang periods that was discovered in Liaoning, several sites that have produced Shang and Zhou bronzes, and bronze daggers and swords that accom-panied burials, etc.

A Western Zhou dynasty bronze utensil – a lei *(a kind of ancient wine vessel) with a lid and coiling dragons pattern.*

Liao ceramics collected by the Liaoning Provincial Museum.

Rooms 3 and 4: Show items from the period of Warring States, Qin, and Han.

Rooms 5, 6, and 7: Show items from the Three Kingdoms, the East and West Jin, the North and South dynasties. Most importantly, on exhibit here are the tomb wall paintings of Liaoyang.

Room 8: Is the exhibition hall for Sui, Tang, and the Five dynasties. The main objects on display were excavated from a Tang-dynasty grave discovered in Chaoyang, also a group of artifacts from the Bohai Kingdom, which include a group of rarely seen earthen statues.

Rooms 9 to 12: Are exhibitions for Liao, Song, Jin, and Western Xia. A key emphasis is the exhibition of items from some extraordinary Liao tombs. Also on display is a farmer's house site from the Jin dynasty, as well as Liao, Song, and Jin ceramics.

Rooms 13 to 18: Exhibit Yuan, Ming and Qing objects. These include Ming-dynasty maps, an inscription from a military commander of the Ming, from eastern Liaoning, also Ming- and Qing-dynasty ceramics and paintings.

A copper gui *called 'yufu* gui,*' a kind of food vessel used in the Western Zhou dynasty unearthed in Kazuo, Liaoning.*

In addition to the above exhibitions, a corridor of stelaes has been set up on the east side of the exhibition hall. This preserves a collection of tomb stones set up from the Han to the Ming dynasties, as well as inscription-stelaes, stone portraits, stone coffins and so on, altogether some one hundred stone objects. One of the important pieces is a Northern-Wei inscription by a famous calligrapher of the time who lived from 386-534 AD.

Contributions of China's National Minorities

China includes people of many nationalities. The special characteristics of each of these ethnic groups have contributed to the tapestry that constitutes Chinese civilization. The following sections describe some of the museums located around China that display their contributions.

Cultural Palace of Minorities

◆ Address: Beijing, Fuxingmennei Dajie, #49

◆ Webpage: http://www.bjmuseumnet.org/museum/mzwhg/one.html

The Cultural Palace of Minorities is located on the west end of Chang'an Street, in Beijing. This is a focal point where all the nationalities of the country can come together for cultural exchange: it is a microcosm of the greater family of diverse peoples that make up China. The building occupies some 30,000 square meters and is a multistoried tower-like structure. It stands 13 stories high and has two wings that flank the central hall.

Some 30,000 objects constitute the collections of the Museum, including scripts, costumes, and handicrafts that relate to minority peoples. The territory from which they are drawn extends to Tibet, Xinjiang, Inner Mongolia, Guangxi, Ningxia, Yunnan and Guizhou. The material encompasses artifacts from all 56 of modern China's ethnic minorities. It also includes historical objects from peoples who once lived on the same territories including Xiongnu, Dangxiang, Qidan, Dian peoples among others. Traditional clothes are a particularly striking part of the collection. There is also a wealth

The exterior of the Cultural Palace of Minorities in Beijing.

A corner of minorities' cultural exhibition hall in Cultural Palace of Minorities in Beijing.

Minorities' garments displayed in the Cultural Palace of Minorities in Beijing.

of religious artifacts relating to every kind of religion in China. Among the objects from Tibet are scriptures, documents, laws, treaties and books that constitute an invaluable historical record.

Historical relics are also held in this museum. They include musical instruments dating to the Tang dynasty, armor from the Yuan dynasty, items from the Western Xia, weapons from the Qing dynasty, and so on.

Based on these collections, the Museum has held exhibitions of ancient scripts, costumes, bronze drums, and a great diversity of other topics. As an example, an exhibition of the Tong minority of Guizhou showed local architecture using not only actual objects but models of architectural sites. It brought in young Dong boys and girls to dance, play instruments, and perform so that the audience could feel they were situated in the deep mountain passes of the Dong people.

An extensive library of books in twenty-four different national minority languages is located in the basement of the Museum. The languages include Han, Mongolian, Tibetan, Korean, Uighur, Kazakh, and others, in some 400,000 volumes. Among these are rarely seen scripts, and artistic works of great value in the form of golden sutras, carved woodblocks, manuscripts, paintings and early rubbings. These have scientific as well as artistic value, in narrating the history of the cultures of all of China's people.

42

Shenyang Palace Museum

◆ Address: Liaoning Province, Shenyang City, Shenhe District, Shenyang Road, #171
◆ Website: http://www.chnmuseum.com/sygg

The Shenyang Palace Museum is located at thecenter of Jing-zi Dajie Center in Shenyang City, Liaoning Province. It covers 60,000 square meters and is a history museum with collections and exhibits that deal mainly with Qing-dynasty art and artifacts.

Formerly called the Fengtian Palace Museum, then the National Shenyang

A panorama of the East Way of the Shenyang Palace Museum displaying Manchu tent-style architectural features.

43

The Dazheng Hall in the Shenyang Palace Museum.

Museum, in 1954 it was officially renamed the Shenyang Palace Museum. In 1961, the State Council placed it among the ranks of National Key Cultural Relics Protected Units. The permanent exhibits of the museum are divided into two parts, one showing historical artifacts of the court and the other showing Qing-dynasty arts and crafts.

The Shenyang Palace Museum is the only well preserved group of ancient palace buildings in the country except for the Beijing Palace Museum. The complex is divided into three parts, the Eastern Way, the Central Way, and the Western Way. The architecture of the main building of the Eastern Way is characteristic of a horse-riding arrow-shooting people who used tent palaces; this Dazheng Hall once hosted tremendous ceremonies.

The main building of the Central Way was where the emperor held daily meetings with his court to conduct governmental affairs and receive ministers. Inside, objects are arranged as they were during the Qianlong period. Inside a separate hall to the west are objects used by the

The Wensu Hall in the Shenyang Palace Museum.

The Phoenix Tower in the Shenyang Palace Museum.

The main gate of the Shenyang Palace Museum.

emperors Qianlong and Jiaqing as these two emperors made their long investigative trips through the country.

On the western side of the Shenyang Palace Museum are riding grounds where horses were kept and trained, also a pavilion in which the emperor watched plays when he did his 'eastern sojourn.' There is also a reconstruction of a Ming-dynasty pavilion from Ningbo, which is one of the seven halls in the Qing dynasty to receive a copy of the famous Yongle-period encyclopedia known as the Siku Quanshu, or the Four Warehouses of All Knowledge.

Most of the Shenyang Palace Museum collections of documents and artifacts date from the Qing dynasty, though some are from the Ming. Many are of interest for their historical value but some are of great artistic value as well, such as paintings by Dong Qichang (1555-1636), a famous Ming painter and calligrapher. Some of the more representative treasures that have been exhibited from the collections of the Museum are Qing-dynasty weapons, musical instruments, palace accouterments, ceramics, carvings, textiles and embroideries, lacquerware, and amber.

The original throne display in the Dazheng Hall.

Inner Mongolia Autonomous Region Museum

◆ Address: Inner Mongolia Autonomous Region, Hohhot City, Xinhua Dajie, #2
◆ Website: http://www.chnmuseum.com/js/nmg.html

This museum was founded on the occasion of the tenth anniversary of the establishment of the Inner Mongolia Autonomous Region, in 1957. The building, expressive of local minority characteristics, is located at the intersection of Xinhua Dajie and Zhongshan Lu in the heart of Hohhot City, the capital of the autonomous region.

The exterior of the Inner Mongolia Autonomous Region Museum.

The Museum holds 44,000 objects relating to ethnic history in its collections. Among these quite a few are rare treasures seldom seen in China, especially the artifacts relating to the northern tribes called Xiongnu, Xianbei, Qidan, Mongolians and others. There are also a large number of cultural relics relating to northern people's living and customs. The Inner Mongolia Museum is a regional-level museum. One of the important sources of its collections are precious materials excavated from the earth as a result of archaeological research. These materials are one of the great specialties of the Museum.

This museum has also been active in collecting and preserving contemporary items that relate to the rich local

The fossil skeleton of a mammoth displayed in the Inner Mongolia Autonomous Region Museum.

An eagle-shaped gold crown of the Warring States period.

culture. At present, there are more than 3,000 sets of such objects, which reflect the lifestyles and customs of a wide variety of Mongolian and other ethnic groups in the region. Among these, notable attractions include the costumes of Mongolian women from different parts of Inner Mongolia as well as Mongolian religious artifacts.

Inner Mongolia is also known as the 'Land of Fossils.' Specimens shown in the museum include massive dinosaurs, mastodons, and many other kinds of fossilized remains from the Mesozoic period that have attracted global attention.

Xinjiang Uighur Autonomous Region Museum

◆ Address: Xinjiang Uighur Autonomous Region, Urumchi, Xibei Road, #132
◆ Website: http://www.chnmuseum.com/js/xjwwe.htm

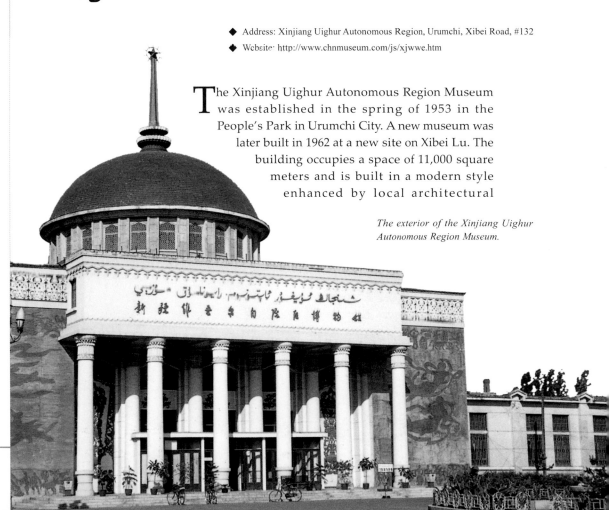

The Xinjiang Uighur Autonomous Region Museum was established in the spring of 1953 in the People's Park in Urumchi City. A new museum was later built in 1962 at a new site on Xibei Lu. The building occupies a space of 11,000 square meters and is built in a modern style enhanced by local architectural

The exterior of the Xinjiang Uighur Autonomous Region Museum.

features. The central dome is thirty meters high and from its height one can view the entire city of Urumchi.

The Silk Road derived its fame from silk. The Xinjiang Uighur Autonomous Region Museum has also become famous for its rich collections of silk artifacts from many periods of history. Brocades from Eastern Han are highlighted, as well as all kinds of specialized silk-woven items from the height of the Tang. These are as lustrous and beautiful today as when they were new and display weaving techniques that were highly refined many hundreds and even thousands of years ago. These are regarded as unique treasures by textile authorities and art historians around the world. A number of the articles on display here are the earliest extant examples of certain weaving technologies in China.

The Xinjiang Autonomous Region has long been a crossroads for many different kinds of people. Their diversity of scripts and cultures is exhibited in this museum through archaeological material, including documents in some twelve different scripts with a particularly large number from the Han-dynasty finds at Turfan. The documents cover military, economic, cultural, and political affairs. Clay or terracotta sculptures are also featured in the Xinjiang Museum. Among these are single-humped Central Asian camels, fat and vigorous Yuan-dynasty horses, women figurines in all postures, impressively fierce soldiers, and so on. These were sculpted in a most

The 'Hu King' brocade unearthed from Astana ancient tombs in Turpan.

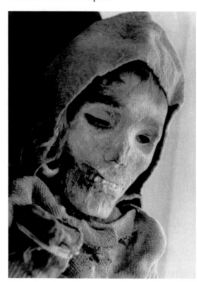

A Loulan female corpse of more than 4,000 years ago unearthed in the Silk Road.

A corner of the Uighur courtyard and house displayed in the Xinjiang People's Customs Exhibition Hall.

natural and vigorous way and have been preserved as a result of Xinjiang's arid climate.

The Xinjiang Museum has several dozen original Tang-dynasty paintings. Although these are not from the hands of famous painters, they still exhibit the vital Tang spirit. They include such subjects as women playing *weiqi* go or Chinese chess, children frolicking, 'eight steeds,' people dancing and so on.

Other items in the collections include microliths, silver works of art, stone stelaes, coins and currency, ceramics, wooden articles. Of particular note are various foods from the Tang dynasty which, through the arid conditions, have been preserved over the passage of more than one thousand years.

In a similar vein, certain dessicated human corpses, called mummies although they were not treated with chemicals, are kept in the Xinjiang Museum. Some of these date back to 4,000 years ago. They are the earliest known such examples in China and are important in the study not only of humankind but of ethnic composition in this region at the time. Also in the museum are an Eastern-Han couple, buried together and well preserved, and a corpse from the Tang dynasty with well preserved skin and hair.

Presently, the museum opened new exhibits called the Xinjiang History Exhibition and the Xinjiang People's Customs Exhibition. The history exhibit shows the history of Xinjiang by using material from its rich collections and highlighting material from recent archaeological discoveries. The Customs exhibition introduces the customs and cultural lifestyles of twelve different ethnic groups in Xinjiang, including the Uighur, Kazakh, Mongolian, Kirgiz, Hui, Tajik, Uzbek, Russian, Tatar, Daur, Xibo, and Manchu.

Tibet Museum

◆ Address: Tibet, Lhasa City, Southeast of Norbulingka
◆ Website: http://www.tibet.cn/tibetzt/xzbwg

The Tibet Museum was officially inaugurated in October of 1999, with a permanent collection that celebrates the History of Tibetan Culture. The design of the exhibit uses traditional Tibetan architecture such as Tibetan doors, beam-decoration, patterns and so on, in order to create the atmosphere of authentic Tibetan art.

The History of Tibetan Culture Exhibition incorporates superb examples of several thousand years of Tibetan history, politics, religion, cultural arts, and customs. It 'takes Tibetan history as the main thread and Tibetan culture as the center' in exhibiting the long history of the Tibetan people and their vast and deep culture. At the same time most of the historical objects also express the fact that Tibet is an inalienable part of Chinese territory.

This exhibit displays around 1,000 precious objects, in a space totaling around 3,000 square meters and with an exhibition line of around 600 meters. The contents are divided into pre-history culture, indivisable history, culture and arts, and people's

The exterior of the Tibet Museum.

54

customs.

Prehistory

This covers a period that stretches back fifty thousand years to three thousand years before the present. The Karuo and Qugong sites are representative of the Neolithic in Tibet. With a large number of characteristic stone tools, pottery, bone objects and metal objects, this exhibition expresses the life of the ancient people of the Tibetan plateau. It also shows the cultural origins of the precursors of the Tibetan people, and their connections with the central plains civilization and Indus River civilization.

Indivisable History

The seal of Yuan emperor's teacher displayed in the Tibet Museum.

This section includes material on different dynastic periods of Tibetan history, including Tibetan regional powers. Its main section revolves around the relationship between the Chinese central government and the Tibetan regional powers and discusses friendly relations between Han and Zang or Tibetan people. A large number of historically valuable objects are displayed as well as cultural relics that have political significance. These include seals, books, official documents, and so on, that clearly indicate the cordial relations that Han and Tibetan people have long enjoyed and the bonds of friendship due to the effective governance of Tibet by successive dynasties in China. It proves that Tibet has been an inalienable part of China since the Yuan dynasty.

Cultural Arts

This is divided into eight segments that include the development of Tibetan-script books, documents and scrolls, the arts of Tibetan theater, Tibetan musical instruments, Tibetan medicine, Tibetan astronomy and calendar reckoning, Tibetan sculpture, and thanka or painting arts. Altogether, these depict an artistic and cultural overview of the last thousand years of Tibetan arts and thoroughly display the once-glorious peaks of Tibetan arts and culture. The exhibited artifacts are treasures of the Tibetan Autonomous Region Cultural Relics Protection Organization that was set up after the establishment of the PRC. Some of these treasures are unique and being shown to the world for the first time; they are historical evidence of the history of Tibetan civilization.

People's Culture

This part of the exhibition is divided into six segments, that include displays of Tibetan people's costumes, items of daily life, arts and handicrafts, means of communication and so on. From a variety of perspectives, these show how Tibetan people dressed, what they ate, how they lived, their marriage and funeral customs, and so on. The exhibits also reflect the friendly relations of Tibetan people with those on their borders, including the influence of Han culture on Tibetan culture and the mutual influence and interpenetration of these two traditions.

An embroidered thanka displayed in the Tibet Museum.

Guangxi Zhuang Autonomous Region Museum

◆ Address: Guangxi Zhuang Autonomous Region, Nanning City, National Minority Dajie, #34

◆ Website: http://www.chnmuseum.com/js/gxzz

This museum was established in 1978 on the east side of the People's Square in Nanning City and in 1988 a new People's Cultural Hall was added to it. The entire Museum occupies 56,757 square meters of space with a building space of 22,761 square meters. The exhibition building is a modern structure with southern architectural characteristics, which contains six exhibition halls.

The 'Guangxi Historical Artifacts Exhibition' exhibits all periods of Guangxi history from Primitive Society up to the Opium War (1840-1842), reflecting local culture and the interchange with the Central Plains and neighboring regions and the process of cultural melding and development. The exhibition of the 'Liujiang Man' shows the earliest hominid fossil found to date within the borders of Guangxi. It belongs to the late period of hominids and is the earliest representative of modern man found to date not only inside China but in all of the Southeast Asia region.

Stone tools manufactured in more than one hundred sites have been found in Guangxi. Mesolithic-period polished-blade stone tools and stones with finely wrought holes in them are displayed in

The exterior of the main exhibition building of the Guangxi Zhuang Autonomous Region Museum.

the museum, as well as a wealth of artifacts from the Neolithic period. Neolithic sites are divided into three main types, those in caves, on hills, and on mountain slopes and artifacts are exhibited from all three. Of particular note is a large ceremonial shovel-shaped object that is 66.4 cm in length and 44.8 cm wide. The quality of its manufacture, its size, and its polishing make it a superlative work.

In the Shang and Zhou periods, two tribes who lived in Guangxi began to have political, economic and cultural relations with the Central Plains region. Certain bronze items are evidence of this cultural interchange although there is also evidence that 2,500 years ago, during the late Western Zhou period, Guangxi's ancient inhabitants were creating their own brilliant bronze culture. Items in the Museum that demonstrate this culture include spears, axes, ladles, bells, and many other items found the 'Matou Yuanlongpo' grave in Wuming County. Early inhabitants also achieved a high level of ceramic technology, with firing temperatures of 1150 degrees centigrade. Many such ceramics are on display in the Museum.

Among the bronzes exhibited are some that allow the visitor to understand something of the ancient Guangxi bronze-drum culture. There are more than 300 drums from this culture in the Museum. One such drum is exhibited in a prominent position; other bronzes include a snake-headed frog-patterned vessel called a *zun*, and other items that clearly show the influence of local artistic traditions. A group of iron objects excavated from the Northern Guangxi region indicate that Guangxi had entered the iron-culture stage by the Warring States period. Qin-dynasty evidence in Guangxi attests to a more than two-thousand-year-old practice of systematic canal-making in the region. Han-dynasty objects are primarily excavated from Han-period tombs and indicate that from this time onward the parallel cultures began to merge.

The regional-culture treasures that are exhibited include bronze drums with carved inscriptions, lacquer painted bronze basins, bronze horses, bronze phoenix

Copper phoenix lamps of the Han dynasty unearthed in Hepu, Guangxi. The necks can be turned or taken apart in order to adjust light and clean the ashes in lamp bodies. The lamp body can hold candle smoke or ashes to avoid pollution.

"The ancient bronze drums Exhibit" displayed in the Guangxi Zhuang Autonomous Region Museum.

The ethical relic garden in the Guangxi Zhuang Autonomous Region Museum.

The exhibition hall of Guangxi ethical customs in the Guangxi Zhuang Autonomous Region Museum.

A jade cup of the Western Han dynasty.

lanterns, lacquer eared cups, bamboo flutes, celadon bowls, glass cups and so on. A 'Yellow Dragon' bronze mirror is unique among all Three Kingdom bronze mirrors. An excavated inscribed tablet excavated from a Jin-dynasty grave notes that 'disasters are reigning throughout the land but south of the river all is peaceful.' This reflects the warring conditions on the central plains during the end of the Western-Jin period, whereas Guangxi was relatively peaceful and the economy was developing rapidly.

The 'Ancient Bronze Drums Exhibit' displays representative works of the eight main types of bronze drums from the Spring and Autumn period to the Qing dynasty, together with relevant documents, drawings and models. It narrates the chronological development, distribution, types, uses, and modern usage of bronze drums in the region. One drum of note is the so-called thundercloud-patterned drum, excavated from Beiliu County in Guangxi. It has a diameter of 165 centimeters and weighs 300 kilometers, and to date is the largest bronze drum to have been found.

Another exhibition reflects the customs of the eleven national minorities in Guangxi. It exhibits their costumes, weavings, dying techniques, embroidery and so on, as well as items to do with local festivals. The Ethnic Minorities Cultural Relics Garden is an outdoor exhibition of rooms of national minority customs. This reproduces certain minority-people's architecture, such as the wooden railing buildings of the Zahuang, bamboo structure of Yao, hanging buildings of Miao, homes of Maonan, drum towers, wind and rain bridges of Dong, and other special features of local architectural design.

60

Ningxia Hui Autonomous Region Museum

◆ Address: Ningxia Hui Autonomous Region, Yinchuan City, Jingning Street, #2

The Ningxia Hui Autonomous Region Museum is in the capital of the region, Yinchuan city, in the old city district. It is located in the grounds of the Chengtian Temple and uses the main building of the temple as its central hall. This was built in traditional manner in 1988 on the foundations of a Qing dynasty building; the rest of the buildings are auxiliary halls also built around 1988. Behind these 'front-court' buildings is a courtyard-style building built in the Qing dynasty.

The exterior of the Ningxia Hui Autonomous Region Museum.

Display of houses of Hui nationality in the Ningxia Hui Autonomous Region Museum.

The institution is a comprehensive-style museum that brings together Ningxia historical artifacts, items of people's customs, and art collections that have been passed down through the ages.

Ningxia Historical Artifacts Exhibition

This focuses on articles from local history, from ancient times up to Ming and Qing. It is divided into sections as follows: primitive society, Shang and Zhou, Qin and Han, Sui and Tang, Song and Yuan, Ming and Qing, and mostly displays items that have been passed down through generations. Objects of natural-history interest include fossilized paleontological material. Early archaeological material includes ceramics of the Majiayao culture, and artifacts from all the dynastic periods of China that represent the border regions cultures. From ancient times, the Ningxia

A gold-plating copper ox of the Western Xia dynasty.

region has been a confluence of cultures, a place where many different nationalities and peoples came together. It displays in particular the interaction of people from border regions and people of the central plains. The Ningxia historical exhibitions provide tangible evidence of this rich history.

The Western Xia History Exhibition

This exhibition portrays the historical development of the Xi Xia Kingdom (1038-1227), using excavated Western Xia artifacts combined with historical documents. Yinchuan City was the Kingdom's capital. Western Xia kings, concubines, and aristocracy are buried in the tomb precinct in the eastern ranges of the Helan Mountains. Among the items on display here are architectural materials excavated from Western Xia tombs, plus Western Xia ceramics recovered from ancient kiln sites at Lingwu. Articles reflect the history, culture, arts, architecture, and political system of both Western Xia and Dangxiang tribes.

The Ningxia Hui Minority Peoples' Customs Exhibition

This exhibition displays the customs of the local Hui people. It shows Hui religion, architecture, handicrafts, clothing, eating customs, ceremonies, and wedding and funeral customs.

Exhibition of Stone Rubbings from the Helan Mountains

The Helan Mountains contain a large number of ancient petroglyphs. Rubbings from these, together with color photographs of the designs, show the early presence and activities of northern-steppe nomadic people's customs. These include sacrifices, hunting, herding, and so on.

The Ningxia Museum currently has around 10,000 items in its collections, which are divided into eight major categories. Notable objects include northern grassland culture animal-style bronze ornaments, Western Han gold, silver and bronze ornaments, Tang-dynasty and Western Xia works of art of various kinds, and Yuan and Ming-dynasty gilded-bronze Buddhist sculpture.

Yunnan Provincial Museum

◆ Address: Yunnan Province, Kunming City, May 1 Road, #2
◆ Website: http://www.ynbwg.cn

The Yunnan Provincial Museum is a regional museum, containing around 50,000 objects in its collections. Among these, historical objects account for around 30,000 items of which there are 7,000 bronzes, revolutionary items (7,200), ethnic minorities cultural objects (7,000), handicrafts (4,000). The Museum represents the local minority people in particular, and features arts from the Dali Kingdom as well as other periods of Yunnan history.

A bronze drum unearthed in Wanjiaba of Chuxiong, Yunnan Province.

The Yunnan Historical Objects Exhibition has strong regional characteristics, elements that distinguish the local cultures from the Central Plains Han-Chinese culture. Using a diversity of excavated objects, the exhibition displays the face of ancient Yunnan. Many of the objects in this exhibition have important scientific and artistic value, and provide material evidence of mankind's social development.

Stone Tools

Discoveries from the Yuanmou site in Yunnan are displayed in this exhibition. The fossilized remains of two early hominid teeth, dating from around 1.7 million years ago, were found at the site in 1965. This is the earliest hominid fossil found on the Asian continent to date, and provides extremely important scientific evidence in the research into man's development from primates.

A copper shellfish holding sacrificial utensil of the Western Han dynasty unearthed in Shizhaishan of Jinning, Yunnan Province.

The exterior of the Yunnan Provincial Museum.

65

Bronzes

From the Warring States to the Western Han period, the various peoples of Yunnan were creating a distinctive bronze culture. Bronzes excavated at a place called Wanjiapo include the earliest bronze drums to be excavated in China. Some bronzes from this site have been exhibited in over ten countries around the world, among which are a cow-and-tiger patterned piece that is particularly lively and a cowry-shell container notable for its reflection of slave-society sacrificial practices. Various items reflect the close cultural interaction of Yunnan people with people of the motherland. These include an incense burner that is central-plains in character, a walking lamp, a bronze mirror, a bronze

A shellfish holding utensil of Dian nationality with seven oxen and two tigers pattern unearthed in Jinning, Yunnan Province.

The bronze ware exhibition in the Yunnan Provincial Museum.

"Two leopards biting a pig" of the Western Han dynasty unearthed in Shizhaishan of Jinning, Yunnan Province.

A copper peacock.

spear, Wuzhu coins, and so on. The seal of the King of the Dian Kingdom in particular testifies to the fact that Yunnan was already an indivisible part of China from some 2,000 years ago.

Yunnan Minority Customs and Ornaments Exhibition

This exhibit displays the dress and ornamentation of some 22 national minorities living in Yunnan, including Dai, Bai, Naxi, Hani, Lahu, Jingpo, Blang, De'ang, Lisu, Pumi, Va, Nu, Drung, Achang, and Jino.

Tracing the Tracks
of History

China is an ancient country with an unbroken line of history that extends back some five thousand years. The diverse threads of the historical process have been saved from obscurity by cultural artifacts by which we can glimpse the accomplishments of our forebears.

National Museum of China

◆ Address: Beijing, Tian'anmen Square, East side
◆ Web site: http://www.nmch.gov.cn/default1024.asp

The National Museum of China is located on the east side of Tian'an Men Square. It is the largest comprehensive history museum in China.

Through display of both material and non-material collections and exhibits, it narrates the history created by the ancestors of the Chinese people.

The National Museum is built on the twin foundations of the former China History Museum and the former China Revolutionary Museum in 2003. The new museum is currently undergoing expansion. It has extremely rich collections and the excellence of its exhibits and depth of its research are second to none.

The main gate of the National Museum of China.

China Ancient History Section

A seismograph model.

The National Museum holds the country's most important historical objects. Through China's History Exhibition, these are shown to visitors from both inside and outside China, to display the long history and shining civilization of the Chinese people. At the same time, the museum undertakes education projects, archaeological excavations and scientific research.

The earliest items on display here are the teeth of Yuanmou Man from Yunnan Province, dating back some 1,700,000 years. The most recent are historical artifacts from Xinhai Revolution of 1911.

The Early Society Exhibition starts with ancient inhabitants (around 1,700,000 years ago to 10,000 years ago), then clan society (around 10,000 years ago to 5,000 years ago) and the dawn of civilization (around 5000 to 4000 years ago). In the ancient inhabitants' section you can see China's earliest 'sapiens' called Yuanmou Man, the slightly later Lantian Man, Beijing Man, Jinniushan Man, and also Shandingdong Man. The last had already entered the homo sapiens period. These ancestors wrote the first page in the chapter of China's history. Stone tools that they created, the seeds they collected, bones of the animals that they hunted are all documented in the exhibition cases. The bone-made needle and the teeth and shells that the Shandingdong Man used for jewelry indicate that by his time, mankind had already begun to sew clothing and have an awareness of aesthetics.

From around 10,000 years ago, mankind began to polish stone tools, make ceramics, weave cloth, and engage in other handicrafts production. The distribution of clans also began to be more widespread. In the exhibit, rice kernels from some 8,000 years ago, bone implements of some 7,000 years ago, and the model of a matriarchal village unearthed in Shaanxi Province from some 6,000 years ago can be seen. From around 5,000 years ago, agricultural techniques were well advanced and besides being able to provide for his own basic needs, man was able to produce a certain surplus. This led to a system of private ownership and the development of classes. At this time, special handicraft industries appeared, also the rudiments of writing, cultural arts and religion. In the exhibits, one can see important ritual

A Four-sheep zun of the Shang dynasty.

A ding with the shape of big broad-mouthed receptacle of the Western Zhou dynasty unearthed in Mei County, Shaanxi Province.

implements of the period made from stone and jade.

The slave society was mankind's first class society in history. This period is divided in the exhibition into Xia, Shang, Western Zhou, and Spring and Autumn periods and one that covers all tribes from Xia to Spring and Autumn.

The Xia Dynasty was the first kingdom in Chinese history. Its center of ruling power was the northern part of what is today Henan and the southern part of Shanxi provinces. The Bronze jue excavated from Yanshi in Henan, and the ceramic cup and so on indicate that agriculture was a primary economic activity in the Xia period, while the manufacture of bronzes was already quite developed.

The Shang period was a glorious time of Chinese bronze development. Craftsmen were able to cast very complex shapes and to create highly refined and beautiful inscriptions and ornamentation. The heaviest bronze piece discovered to date is on exhibit here; called the 'Simuwu Ding,' which weighs 832.84 kilograms. A four-ram 'zun' and other representative Shang dynasty bronzes are on display. In addition to bronzes, the manufacture of ceramics, lacquer-making, weaving, jade carving and so on also achieved a certain level of accomplishment. The early-porcelain zun excavated at Zhengzhou in Henan is one of the earliest pieces of porcelain found in China to date. Another notable achievement of the Shang dynasty is the ancient script known as *jiaguwen*, or ancient writing on the shoulder-blade bones of oxen and the front plates of tortoises. This writing began the construction of the basic shapes that later developed into 'Han' characters.

Chinese bronze-making technology flourished during the Western Zhou period, following the Shang. In terms of political organization, China followed a system of divided feudal authority, and a severe system of rites and also punishments was instituted. The ceremonies or rites were used to moderate relations within the ruling class, the system of punishments was used to control and oppress commoners and slaves. Items on display give evidence of these things.

The Spring and Autumn period in China was a period of transition from slave society to feudal society, when the power of the Zhou court greatly declined and some relatively large kingdoms or dukedoms expanded their own influence, initiating a period of intense warfare. The exhibition has representative objects from all the Dukedoms or Kingdoms of the time, and also the world's earliest military tract, excavated in Shandong, called 'Sunzi Bingfa,' which is commonly translated into English as 'the Art of Warfare.'

The final section in this brief review of early Chinese history shows items from the people on the periphery of the central plains region. These objects have a clearly regional or 'outside' quality, and yet they also reflect a relationship between their own locality and the central plains. Representative objects are a dragon-tiger zun from Anhui, an elephant zun from Hunan, and some ancient Shu bronzes excavated from Guanghan in Sichuan.

The many centuries from the Warring States until the Opium Wars (475 BC-1840 AD) is regarded as representing a time of feudal society in China. The feudal society exhibit includes seven parts: the Warring States period, Qin, Han, Three Kingdoms, Western and Eastern Jin, North and South Dynasties, Sui, Tang, Five Kingdoms, Song, Yuan, Ming, and Qing. The feudal society exhibit occupies three-fourths of the total China History Exhibit space.

The Warring States period saw unprecedentedly fierce warfare as local states consolidated, and at the same time was a period of rapid economic growth and cultural development. Bronzes of various kinds and coins from many regions are some of the many items on display here. The Qin period reflects the first unified, multi-ethnic, centralized-power feudal period in Chinese history. The period is portrayed by showing some of the Qin soldiers and horses from the famous pit of the First Emperor of

A big copper mirror with double fish pattern of the Jin dynasty unearthed in Acheng, Heilongjiang Province.

A 12-character-brick in small seal character of the Qin dynasty that reads "All people are subject to me, every field harvests and everyone can have enough food."

Qin, among other items.

To help the visitor understand the power and majesty of the Western Han and the expansive power of the Eastern Han, a number of wall murals, models of sites, and so on are exhibited, together with actual objects from the periods. These show the increasing connections among all continental peoples in the Western Han period.

The Three Kingdoms, Western and Eastern Jins, and North and South Dynasties were, in Chinese history, a tumultuous and unsettled time. Yet they were also a period of great advances. The Three Kingdoms, Wei, Shu and Wu, are exhibited in the form of bronzes and ceramics with the ceramics in particular showing a high level of glazing technology in the south.

The Sui and Tang periods were another time of great unification in Chinese history. The exhibit reflects the feudal economics of the time, also the increasingly close relations between people of the interior and tribes of the periphery. Exhibited works include items excavated from the grave of Li Jingxun, such Tang Sancai ceramics as a camel carrying musicians, finely glazed ceramics such as ding-yao, carved woodblock printed items excavated from Chengdu, and a Guanyin statue of gilded bronze excavated from Zhejiang.

During the Song and Yuan periods, China's feudal society continued to develop and one clear trait was that the contradictions between Han people and minority peoples intensified yet economic and cultural relations were strengthened. This can be seen in the various items on display.

The Ming and Qing dynasties marked the end of the period of Chinese feudal society. The general trend of this period was general decline and decay in the feudal society, for the 543 years from 1368 with the establishment of the Ming dynasty to Xinhai Revolution of 1911 which overturned the Qing dynasty. The main items in the Ming

A Tang-triple-color musical band carrying ceramic camel unearthed in Xi'an, Shaanxi Province.

A model of Liao dynasty wood pagoda of Ying County displayed in the National Museum of China.

and Qing part of the exhibition include a Beijing Palace map, porcelains from the Jingdezhen kilns, a Qing-dynasty jade seal, a painting of the Qianlong emperor's southern tour, textile equipment made in England, and the swearing-in document when Sun Yatsen took office as President, the latter being a reproduction.

73

A haiyan river zun *of the Qing dynasty (Qianlong Period).*

Modern Chinese History Exhibit

This describes how imperialist powers invaded China and also established ties with China's feudal powers, forcing China into a half-colonial half-feudal society. It depicts the resistance of China's people against imperialism, feudalism and the bureaucratic capitalism of Britain. It gives the tortuous path China has taken on its way to modernization.

The Modern China Exhibition is divided into seven parts. In a hall of 2,000 square meters, it uses 2,300 articles including objects, documents, photographs and charts, models, paintings, sculpture and reproductions of sites, simulated environments and so on to produce a lively exhibit of one hundred years of Chinese history from the 1840 Opium War to the establishment of the Chinese People's Republic in 1949. The exhibit reflects the brave struggle and persevering spirit of all levels of people in the search for China's revolutionary path.

The Contemporary China Exhibition will continue the Modern China Exhibit in reflecting contemporary China's historical process.

The evolutional history exhibition on Red Army's Long March.

The historical exhibition on the Revolution of 1911 that overthrew the Qing dynasty.

Sanxingdui Museum

◆ Address: Sichuan Province, Guanghan City, Xiyazi River
◆ Website: http://sxd.cn

The Sanxingdui Museum is near an archaeological site that dates to the Neolithic, Shang and Zhou periods. In 1988 this site was declared a National Key Cultural Relics Protected Unit, due to its scope, the wealth of its contents, and the rarity and precious nature of its excavated objects.

The site is north of Nanxing Town of Guanghan City in Sichuan Province. It is mainly located on the raised platform between the Yazi River and the Mamu River and it covers 12 square kilometers in total area. The most concentrated parts of the site are at the towns of

The external appearance of the Sanxingdui Museum.

Sanxing, Rensheng, Zhenwu, and Huilong.

The artifacts from Sanxingdui have had global influence. In 1986, two large Shang-period sacrificial pits were unearthed with more than one thousand gold, bronze, and jade objects, shocking the entire country and shaking the world. Among other things, the finds proved that Sanxingdui was the capital of the ancient Shu Kingdom more than 3,000 years ago. Of all the objects excavated at Sanxingdui, the bronzes are the most fabulous and strange, with their high degree of historical, artistic and scientific value.

Ceramics: Most of the ceramics unearthed at Sanxingdui are made of 'jiashahe' clay and are made on a wheel. They date mainly from four periods: the first from some 4,800 to 4,000 years ago, during a representative Neolithic period culture in the Sichuan basin, the second is roughly contemporary with Xia to Shang, the third with the late Shang, and the fourth with late Shang to the early Western Zhou. From the shape, decoration, and base and method of manufacture, the above ceramics represent an unbroken line of development of Shu culture.

Jades: Although not numerous, the level of production

Bronze masks.

76

A big bronze standing human statue.

is high and these are well preserved. Among them are ceremonial objects, military objects and tools, with the blades still as sharp as when they were buried. The blades of these objects are so very thin that one can see they were ceremonial in nature and not for actual work or warfare.

Gold objects: Not only were the gold objects excavated from Sanxingdui very finely made but they were quite special. They included face masks and various kinds of ceremonial equipment. Among them, a gold staff, with a human head carved on top with fish, birds, and grain is executed in a fine manner with an extremely beautiful pattern.

Bronzes: The Sanxingdui bronzes have been exhibited both inside and outside China and have shaken the field of art history. The imaginative power of the human statues in particular, their artistic exaggeration, majesty, refinement, and execution make them truly divine works among Shang and Zhou bronzes.

This group of bronzes can roughly be divided into two types. One is ceremonial objects, and from the shape and artistic style we can see similarities to surrounding regions. Another type of bronzes is strongly religious in flavor: these constitute religious statues, or idols. Among them is a statue of a standing man who is 2.62 meters high and weighs 180 kilograms. His nose is high and straight, his eyes are large, his forehead is square and he has large ears from which hang pierced earlobes. A long braid hangs down behind his head; he wears a resplendent tall crown on his head, his body is covered with dragon-and cloud-patterned robe that folds to the left; his left hand is raised, his right arm is folded across his chest, his hands are large, the two feet are bare and he stands on a square pedestal. Among Shang and Zhou bronzes, his shape and manner are absolutely unique.

Bronze heads and face masks were also among the superlative excavated bronzes. Among these, one mask is 134 centimeters wide and 65 centimeters tall and weighs ten kilograms. If one estimates the full height of a statue with these proportions, it would be an awesome four meters. The mask has large ears and high nose, and exaggerated eyes with protruding pupils.

The grounds and environment of the new museum are exceptionally beautiful. The surrounding space is large and is arranged as in a park, with pools, collections of stones, flowers and trees; the setting also borrows from the natural beauty of the nearby streams.

Zhouyuan Museum

◆ Address: Shaanxi Province, Baoji City, Fugang County, Famen Town, Zhaochen Village

Zhouyuan is an ancient region with more than 3,000 years of history. It is located in the western part of the Guanzhong Plain of Shaanxi Province and includes one of the capitals of the early period of the Zhou Dynasty. In history it is known as 'Qi Zhou.' The cultural relics both on and below ground are especially rich, and the large quantity of bronzes excavated here are world famous. In 1982, this was declared by the State Council to be a National Important Cultural Relics Protected Unit.

The Zhouyuan Museum was built on the foundation of the excavation of the Zhouyuan site. It was formerly the site of two cultural relics Protection and Management Institutes called Zhouyuan Qishan and Fugang. In 1986 these were combined to become the Zhouyuan Museum which is located in Fugang County, Famen Town, Zhaochen Village.

The Zhouyuan Museum's existing exhibitions are divided into inside and outside components. The outside exhibitions are mainly the Village Ancestral Temple and the Zhaochen Village Palace, a large-scale architectural grouping. These provide a valuable resource for researching Western Zhou architecture and technology, and the political, economic and cultural systems of the court at that time. These fill what had been a void in ancient Chinese architectural history.

The architectural ruins of Zhaochen Palace in Zhouyuan, Shaanxi.

This wall plate was a bronze ware made in Gong King period of the Western Zhou dynasty. The bottom of the inside body was engraved with inscriptions of 284 characters.

A bronze ware of Zhao King period of the Western Zhou dynasty.

A bronze shang you (wine vessel) of early period of the Western Zhou dynasty.

The inside exhibitions mainly include the Zhouyuan Excavated Relics Exhibit, the Zhouyuan Historical Cultural Relics Exhibit, Western Zhou Calligraphy and Arts Exhibit, Western Zhou Wine-Culture Exhibit, and the special exhibit at Famensi Temple which is called the Zhouyuan Precious Cultural Relics Special Exhibit. These exhibits display the some 3,000 items excavated at the Zhouyuan site, including bronzes, jades, bone, ceramics, augury tortoise shells, augury bones, and so on.

In the exhibition, people can enjoy bronzes from three thousand years ago such as one that has 284 characters inscribed on the bottom of its interior, relating the history of six kings of Western Zhou and the important accomplishments of the currently-in-power seventh king. It also records the family history of the owner of the vessel, providing reliable data for researching Zhou-dynasty

Mini bone inscriptions of the Western Zhou dynasty unearthed in Zhouyuan, Shaanxi Province.

history. In the Western Zhou Wine-Culture Exhibition, around one hundred specimens of materials for fermenting alcohol, vessels for fermentation, articles for warming wine, for mixing alcohols and so on are exhibited. China's earliest ceramic-material architectural tiles are also on display, which date to six to seven hundred years earlier than the Qin bricks and Han tiles of Chinese tradition. In the exhibit people can also see valuable western Zhou *jiaguwen* or oracle bone inscriptions, which record the relations between Zhou people and the Shang court as well as other countries. In the calligraphy section, examples of western Zhou calligraphy that have been excavated in recent years are on display.

Suizhou Zenghouyi Tombsite Exhibition Hall

◆ Address: Hubei Province, Wuhan City, Wuchang District, Donghu Road, #88
◆ Website: http://www.hubeimuseum.net

The Suizhou Zenghouyi Tombsite Exhibition Hall is located in the Hubei Provincial Museum. The Hubei Provicial Museum is on the edge of Wuchang East Lake, a very beautiful place. Since the establishment of the museum, many exhibitions have been held here. The collections currently hold some 200, 000 objects among which the most astonishing are the objects excavated from the Zenghouyi Tomb.

A 'Serial bells' or bianzhong *unearthed in the tomb of Zenghouyi.*

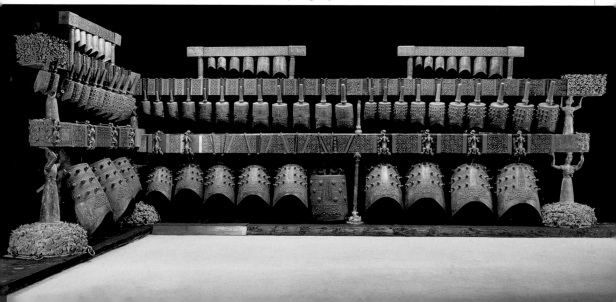

A color painted wood carving table screen unearthed in a Chu tomb.

The Zenghouyi Tomb was built about 2400 years ago. The richness of the objects excavated from this tomb and their exquisite beauty has made them one of the rare sights of the world. The musical instruments alone have been called an underground musical palace. Among these instruments, the *bianzhong* or bells are most famous. There are altogether 65 bells: 19 *niu* bells, 45 *tong* bells, and 1 *fu* bell. The entire set is capable of performing ancient as well as modern music and Chinese as well as all kinds of foreign music since their tonal range is broad and the quality of sound is beautiful. The Hubei Provincial Museum made a special exhibition room for this set of *bianzhong*, and specialists at certain times give performances of ancient music for visitors.

Hubei was the center of Chu culture. Inside the Chu tomb were Chu items but also rare objects from other countries, such as the kingdom of Yue. A sword belonging to the King of Yue is, for example, one of the treasures found in the Chu tomb for the beauty of this sword has long been world famous.

This bronze zun *plate unearthed in the tomb of Zenghouyi deserves to be considered a masterpiece of bronze wares of the Warring States period.*

Qin Shi Huang Terracotta Warriors and Horses Museum

◆ Address: Shaanxi Province, Xi'an City, Lintong County, Qinling Town
◆ Website: http://www.bmy.com.cn

A remarkable sight appeared in 1974, near the ancient capital of Xi'an. Some farmers happened to dig up what turned out to be a large-scale pit with terracotta soldiers and horses, belonging to the Emperor Qin Shi Huang, or the Founding Emperor of the Qin. After 2,200 years, the Emperor's tremendous army stood as though living again before people's eyes.

The figures that the farmers found were around the size of real people. The pit was in Shaanxi Province, Lintong County, Jiangzhai xichang Village. It was around three Chinese *li*, or roughly one mile, from the east side of the Emperor Qin Shi Huang's tomb mound. The Chinese Cultural Relics Administrative Department immediately organized its forces and carried out an investigation. After further

The external appearance of the Qin Shi Huang Terracotta Warriors and Horses Museum.

excavation they actually found that the area of the discovery was a great deal larger and that inside this area were buried some 6,000 terracotta figures of horses and soldiers. After this, archaeologists discovered a second and third pit of horses and soldiers: the first discovery was called #1 pit, nearly in fact excavations they discovered pits #2 and #3. Linked together, the three pits covered an area of 20,000 square meters and included around 8,000 figures.

An archer warrior tomb figure in squatting position.   *An armor-wearing warrior tomb figure.*

To bury an entire army of individual soldiers under the ground was unheard of in the world. This ancient phenomenon gave evidence to the world of the Chinese people's sophistication and rich cultural heritage. It is no wonder that the former French Premier expressed amazement when he saw it, 'The Qin terracotta pit is one of the marvels of the world. To go to Egypt and not see the pyramids is not really going to Egypt; to go to China and not see this sight is not really going to China.'

In order to better protect this historical treasure house, a building was put over the #1 pit which has a bow-shaped steel framework, to form a vast exhibition hall. The building is 230 meters long, 72 meters wide, and 22 meters

A separate line of foot soldiers in #1 pit.

The copper horses and horse cart.

The battle array in #1 pit.

Terracotta Horses.

high. It can hold two football fields inside. The Qin Shi Huang Terracotta Warriors and Horses Museum was officially inaugurated and opened to the public in 1979.

Standing inside the hall over #1 pit, people can see over 1,000 of the horses and soldiers that have been excavated and cleaned up; the rest of the 5,000 are in the process of being cleaned, one by one. The army is arrayed in a rectangular formation, all facing east. In front are three rows each with 210 warriors making up the front ranks, after them are marching soldiers and horses drawing war chariots, making up the main body of this army. The two sides of the army and the rear each have a line of warriors, divided to face south, north, west – this was perhaps to maintain a contingent for the sides and the rear of the hall, to guard against rear attack.

The terracotta statues, horses and people, are roughly the same size as real horses and people, the proportions are extremely accurate. This reflects the high level of sculptural arts at the time of the Qin dynasty. From the placement, the hair and clothing styles and weaponry of the statues, one can generally understand their rank and position. Some wear tunics, some carry shields, some have their hair tied in a bun, some wear footwear while others do not, some have armor breastplates, some have fishscale armour. Soldiers with relatively long beards are placed towards the rear, and one sees at a glance that they are seasoned older generals. In addition to foot soldiers there are also some cavalry members leading horses or driving chariots. Some of the soldiers are kneeling, ready to shoot their arrows: each has a special posture according to his duties.

Overlooking the Qin Shi Huang Tomb.

In terms of finer features, the statues are remarkably lifelike. The head and facial expression of each soldier is different, so that clearly each was the work of a sculptor and they were not produced from a mold. Through fine detail on the eyebrows, face, mouth and nose, the internal character and rich expressions of each soldier are expressed. Some of the statues were clearly northwest minority peoples, which also shows the origins of the Qin-dynasty soldiers.

The cavalry and war chariots had an extremely important place in ancient armies. Those examples excavated from the pit included steeds that were vigorous and fat. Their ears were erect, their eyes wide and mouths open, they were generally 1.5 high, with smallish heads and relatively short legs. Some people say that these horses seem to resemble the Hequ Horses found in Gansu today or the Hetian Horses found in Xinjiang, which are excellent racehorses, good at climbing slopes, and also are excellent warhorses with great strength.

During the Warring States period, seven powers were at continual war with each other and the competition among their leaders led to a great advances in weapons' design and production. By the time of the establishment of the Qin dynasty, weapons were quite sophisticated. Before this pit was discovered, when people saw only single examples of Qin weapons, this was not believed to be the case. Once the pit was uncovered and a large number of actual weapons were unearthed, people began to recognize the martial and organizational capabilities of the Qin-dynasty army. Every one of the statues unearthed in the pit had a weapon, and all were actual weapons made of bronze. At the time, the three great kinds of cold weapons (as opposed to what Chinese call hot weapons which came only after the invention of gunpowder) were distant firing weapons, such as bows and arrows, weapons for close-in combat and longer weapons for less close combat. All of these were represented in the pit.

What is most amazing is that these weapons were still sharp and shiny after being excavated. Having been buried over 2,000 years, they had not rusted, except for those that had been crushed and damaged. After rubbing away the mud and dirt one could see that they were shiny, making one think they had just come from a Qin-dynasty craftsman's hands. The production of these weapons was very careful, including cold-casting treatment added to the surface. The weapons were of an alloy made of copper, tin, and lead but the percentages were different for different categories of weapons and there were microquantities of different elements to allow for different hardnesses and elasticity needs. Qin-dynasty craftsmen were in possession of very high metallurgical technology. The blades of the weapons had an oxidized layer and after scientific evaluation it was seen that they were put through a salt oxidizing process. This treatment of the surface is a modern technology that was already in use in Chinese weapons production some 2,000 years ago. This thin layer of protection is what kept the weapons from rusting despite being buried for so long.

More than ten thousand bronze weapons were unearthed from Qin terracotta figure pits and this is a long handle weapon used at that time called 'ji.'

Changsha Mawangdui Han Tomb Cultural Relics Exhibition Hall

◆ Address: Hunan Province, Changsha City, Dongfeng Road, #3

This museum is located in Hunan Province and the tombs and objects that it exhibits date back 2,000 years. Exhibited here are some 3,000 objects from three separate tombs containing the senior Minister of the State of Chu, his wife, and son. The articles excavated from the tomb have been highly important in researching this very wealthy and sophisticated southern-Chinese culture.

The first room of the Museum exhibits lacquer ware, bamboo and wooden objects, agricultural implements, musical instruments, military implements, wooden figures, silk woven articles and clothes, in addition to three large coffins, together with their covering paintings, books, bamboo slips, and so on. Among the lacquers excavated from the #3 tomb are cups, saucers, boxes, kettle, tables,

The external appearance of the exhibition hall built to display and preserve relics excavated from Mawangdui Han Tomb in the Hunan Provincial Museum.

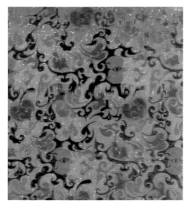

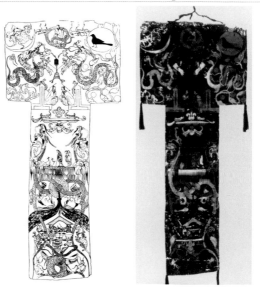

*A piece of "riding clouds embroidery"
unearthed from Western Han tombs in
Mawangdui, Hunan Province.*

*Brocade paintings unearthed from
#1 tomb in Mawangdui, Changsha.*

screens, and a variety of other objects, totaling some 500 pieces altogether. Among them, most were items of daily use for the lady Xin Zhui while she was alive. These objects had been buried for 2,000 years, and yet are as freshly colored and complete today as when they were new. The #1 tomb produced 48 bamboo cases in which all kinds of agricultural products, fruit, meat, Chinese herbal medicines and so on were packed. Wild game predominated among the varieties of meat. Both #1 and #3 tombs produced a large amount of silk material and these were analyzed by authorities and included such weave types as sha, luo, jiun, min, qi, and so on, all of which has great value for the research of ancient Chinese textiles. Ancient Chinese describe silk fabrics as 'thin as dragonfly wings, light as fog' and two pieces excavated from #1 tomb, one weighing 48 grams, the other 49 grams, live up to that description.

The family that was entombed in this place was aristocratic. They listened to music in particular, for the musical instruments excavated from the tomb included lutes, bells, flutes, and bi. The bi is an ancient Chinese stringed instrument and the one excavated from #1 tomb had 25 strings. The instruments provide important historical material for researching ancient Chinese music.

The occupant of Tomb #3 was a military general. Many weapons were excavated from this tomb but there were also some twenty varieties of books, including altogether some 100,000 characters. Among the books were volumes one and two of 'Laozi,' and the Spring and Autumn Annals, and so on. The earliest volumes of

The well preserved corpse of the tomb owner (Xin Zhui) of #1 tomb.

Black lacquer coffins.

most of these had long since been lost, so the recovery of these early texts has tremendous scholarly value. Among the written materials, a map is a particular treasure as it reflects the quite sophisticated early Chinese understanding of geographic drawing.

The inner coffin of both Xin Zhui's and her son's coffins was covered with a T-shaped piece of painting, which in ancient times was called a *mingsheng*. On these pieces of fabric were extremely fine paintings. The conceptual layout of the painting on #1 tomb's fabric was a tripart division into heaven, the human realm, and under the earth. The colors of the painting are fresh, the strokes are fluid and this is considered a masterpiece among ancient art.

Before the Western Han period, China practiced a two-layered coffin system, by which there was an inner and outer coffin. Since Xin Zhui was married to very high rank, she used a four-layered kind of coffin. The inner coffins were painted. The second layer of the coffin was the most beautiful with black background painted with scenes of heaven including strange spirits and peculiar animals floating about.

In the second exhibition room one can see the 2,000-year-old female corpse excavated from #1 tomb. All kinds of measures were adopted during her burial, including burying the coffin very deeply and sealing it tightly so that the coffin lacked oxygen as fuel for bacteria. The corpse therefore still had hair, its joints were limber and the soft organs were still soft. At the end of 1972, medical research was carried out on the corpse. The blood-type of the lady was A-type; during her lifetime she suffered from both lung and heart disease.

A visit to this Mawangdui Exhibition Hall will allow the visitor to understand an aristocrat's life at the time of the western Han dynasty. Not only can one see the actual artifacts, but one can begin to understand the politics, economics, cultural and scientific technologies of the time. It is as though one were reading an encyclopedia on the Western Han period.

Treasures of China's Stone Grottoes

China's world-famed grottoes can be thought
of as an extended art gallery of ancient sculpture,
wall paintings, and sutras. Although this gallery is
not called a 'museum,' still it holds some of the
rarest and most precious works of art in the world.

92

Dunhuang Mogao Grottoes

◆ Address: Gansu Province, Dunhuang City, Mingsha Mountain, East Ridge

The Dunhuang Mogao Grottoes are located in Dunhuang County, Gansu Province, some twenty-five kilometers southeast of the city. The common name for the grottoes is the Thousand-Buddha caves. These are located on the precipitous face of the east ridge of the Mingsha Mountains. Their construction began in the year 366 AD and, by the time of the Tang-dynasty empress named Wu Zetian, more than one thousand rooms had been carved and painted. Those that have been preserved to this day include rooms from the dynasties of Northern Wei, Western Wei, Northern Zhou, Sui, Tang, Five Dynasties, Song, Westerm Xia, and Yuan. In all there are some 492 grottoes, with wall paintings covering 45,000 square meters, and containing 2,415 painted stone carvings. This is considered a priceless artistic trove. It is now protected as a National Key Cultural Relics Protected Unit, and in 1987 it was listed among the ranks of World Cultural Heritage Sites.

The #16 grotto at Dunhuang is the one that attracted global attention and brought treasure seekers from the West. Two Song-dynasty paintings

The external appearance of the Mogao Grottoes.

The huge mural painting of the Tang dynasty in the #156 grotto: Dunhuang Heroes Zhang Yichao Couple Going on a Journey.

The mural painting Female Performers Playing Music *full of flavors of human world in the #122 grotto, and 'reverse-playing pipa' is considered the consummate skill among musical dance performances.*

on its walls show Bodhisattvas on a journey. This is the latest evidence of use of the cave and from this it can be surmised that around the beginning of the eleventh century, when the Western Xia people invaded this area and conquered Dunhuang, monks at the Mogao Grottoes prepared to flee. They sealed the cave and never returned. For nine hundred years, the room was silently shut off from the world. In the year 1900, when the passageway was being cleaned of debris, this stone archive full of sutras, books, embroideries and sculpture was suddenly discovered. It had some 50,000 items in it and these were later found to include not only a large number of Buddhist sutras, but also Daoist works and works of the Confucian canon, in addition to historical records, poetry, literature, information on geography, population, business accounts, calendars and so on. It was discovered to be

A Dunhuang Buddha figure in nirvana.

a full library containing material that documented some ten dynasties, from the Jin in the 4th century to the Song dynasty.

The discovery of the hidden 'sutra cave' was a tremendous and startling event for both Chinese and foreign scholars around the world. It attracted extreme attention and as a result was quickly plundered by scholars from England, France, America, Russia, and Japan. In 1943 a Dunhuang Arts Academy was established which began to restore the cave and protect and research its remaining contents.

There are five levels in all to the Mogao Grottoes, which range from north to south across roughly 1,600 meters. The largest grottoes are 40 meters high and 30 meters square. The smallest are less than one foot. Dunhuang studies have become an established field of scholarship in many

Painted sculptures in the Thousand Buddha Grotto.

96

A profile of the plank road of the Thousand Buddha Grotto.

institutions by now, and countless numbers of books and PhD theses have been written about the history and artwork of this extraordinary place. Rather than try to cover the scope of this 'museum' here, the reader is encouraged to go and see for himself.

The silk painting of the guiding Bodhisattva discovered in the Scripture Hiding Grotto.

Yungang Grottoes

◆ Address: Shanxi Province, Datong City, Western Suburbs, Southern Ridge of Wu Zhou Mountain

The three main sites in China that are famous for their stone sculpture are Dunhuang, Longmen and Yungang. Among these, the Yungang grottoes are considered first among equals, for their tremendous size, their ancient history, and their relatively complete state of preservation. In 1961, the State Council of China declared this a National Key Cultural Relics Protected Unit, and in 2001 the site was listed as a World Cultural Heritage Site.

The grottoes are located 16 kilometers to the west of Datong City in Shanxi Province, on the southern ridge of Wu Zhou Mountain. They were carved into the mountain and extend for a kilometer in length. Their carving began in the first year of the Northern Wei dynasty, or 460 AD, and most of the work was finished

The main gate of the Yungang Grottoes.

A Bodhisattva figure.

Buddha statues on all sides. The carvin in these two grottoes is very practiced and is considered to represent the pinnacle of the art at Yungang.

West Portion of the Grottoes

To the west of the #20 grotto are relatively small caves, some of which have not yet been given numbers. Right now they number #21 to #53. The dating of these is relatively late, most being works after the 19th year of Emperor Tai He of Northern Wei (495). The carving styles and techniques are more developed than in the eastern and central sections, the Buddha figures are thinner and so on. This is a more Sinified style of Buddhist art, which begins to approach the style of Longmen after the capital of the Northern Wei moved to Luoyang.

The Yungang Grottoes are an open-air museum that attracts the attention of thousands of scholars from around the world every year. The historic and artistic value of the art here is of the highest level.

Longmen Grottoes

◆ Address: Henan Province, to the south of Luoyang City

The well-known 'Tablet of Yique Buddhist Shrine.'

The Longmen Grottoes are located sixteen kilometers south of Luoyang in Henan province, on the banks of the Yi River. They constitute a world-renowned artistic treasure, now protected as a National Key Cultural Relics Protected Unit and listed as a World Cultural Heritage Site in 2000. The grottoes were begun in the year 494 AD, around the time the Northern Wei Emperor Xiao Wen moved the capital to Luoyang. The caves then passed through some 400 years of carving and construction, through the dynasties of East and West Wei, Northern Qi, Sui, Tang, and Northern Song. The grottoes honeycomb the mountains.

Altogether there are more than 2,100 grottoes at Longmen, with more than 100,000 statues, some 3,600 inscriptions and stelaes, and forty Buddha's stupas. The finest grottoes are the Northern Wei-period Guyang Grotto, the Binyang Grotto, the Lianhua Grotto, and the Tang-dynasty Qianxi Temple, among others. Some of the stelaes and inscriptions have become treasures among China's calligraphic arts, including the Tang-dynasty calligraphed work by Chu Suiliang (596-659).

The elaborate works of the Longmen Grottoes.

The Binyang Grotto is on the northern part of Longmen Mountain and is composed of three caves. The middle one was begun around 500 AD and was finished in 520, so took twenty-four years to complete. It is recorded that 802,366 craftsmen worked on this grotto. The central Buddha or Sakyamuni and two Bodhisatvas have long, thin faces, and the folds of their clothing is very fine, a characteristic of Northern Wei art. The Lotus-flower or Lianhua Grotto was built in the late Northern Wei period. Its main Sakyamuni is standing and is 5.1 meters tall. The cave is carved with architectural details and floral designs, with scrolling grass patterns, lotus flowers, Baoxiang flowers and so on, all very finely carved. A large lotus flower is carved in high relief on the ceiling.

The statues of the Hercules and King of Heaven near the north wall of the Fengxian Temple.

The Yaofang Grotto, which depicts medicinal cures, is in the northern part of Longmen Mountain. It was begun in the late Northern Wei period and was finished during the Tang-dynasty period of Empress Wu Zetian, so construction lasted around two hundred years. This is the only relatively large cave at Longmen that has Northern Qi statues. Some 140 different kinds of medicines and treatments of various illnesses are carved on either side of the cave entryway, which are very important research material for study of China's ancient pharmacopeia.

The Fengxian Temple is at the southern end of Longmen Mountain. It was begun in 672 and completed over the next four years. This contains representative works of Tang-dynasty carving arts. The Buddha is huge, and is accompanied by eleven sculptures including disciples, Bodhisatvas, the King of Heaven, Guards and so on. According to the inscription on the sculptures, Wu Zetian helped finance the construction with twenty-thousand 'guan' of money, and personally participated in leading ministers in the ceremony of 'opening the light,' i.e. opening the eyes of the Buddha. There is a large stone on the east bank of the Yi River, commonly called the beating-the-drum rock, which is said to be where Wu Zetian played music at the time of the ceremony.

The main Buddha Lushena and his Bodhisattva in the Fengxian Temple in the Longmen Grottoes.

Dazu Carvings

◆ Address: Chongqing City, Dazu County

The Dazu stone carvings at Chongqing are one of ancient China's most valuable treasures. They were declared a National Key Cultural Relics Protected Unit in 1961, and in 1999 they were listed as a World Culture Heritage Site.

These carvings are distributed over 41 places in Dazu County, Sichuan. Some 50,000 carvings were begun in 892 AD and carved in the ensuing Five Dynasties and Northern and Southern Song, or over a span of some 250 years. In addition to Buddhist and Daoist art, there are also Buddhist, Daoist, and Confucian statues that stand together in one grotto of which the 'Mimony' or Tantric (esoteric) Buddhist statues predominate. The largest concentration and largest scale of carvings are at Baoding and Beishan.

The Baoding carvings are to the northeast of Dazu City, amongst beautiful mountains. Buddhist disciples have traditionally brought incense to the sacred place and there is a saying 'look up towards Emei, look down towards Baoding.' The Song-dynasty Emperor Zhao Zhifeng was the instigator of the many Buddhist carvings in this region. Some thirteen places on

A thousand-hand Guanyin Bodhisattva statue on Baoding Mountain in Dazu.

A Guanxin in charming manner.

娟态观音

Breast-feeding.

the mountains hold around ten thousand sculptures that were accomplished over seventy years, from 1179 to 1249. The largest in scale are the Great Buddha Bay and the Small Buddha Bay. In addition to displaying Song-dynasty sculptural art, these are of interest for their narrative appeal: they tell about the birth of Buddha, about the nature of change, about heaven, hell, cause and effect, and especially about people. Normal people, including farmers, are shown working in the carvings, also singing and dancing, drinking wine, pursuing the various tasks of daily life.

A chicken raising lady.

The sleeping Buddha in the Dazu Stone Carving Site.

Underground Imperial Palaces

The tombs of emperors are a microcosm of the life of the occupant. Objects excavated from them are a kind of living fossil of the history of ancient society. The following section presents only the more famous of the extraordinary number of such microcosms buried in the earth of China.

110

Tomb of the Yellow Emperor

◆ Address: Shaanxi Province, Huangling County

The tablet of the Yellow Emperor Tomb in Qiaoshan.

The Chinese traditional understanding is that the ancestor of the Chinese people is called the Yellow Emperor, and that this Yellow Emperor is buried in the heartland of early China, in what is now the province of Shaanxi. One particular county in Shaanxi lays claim to the burial place of this august being: in 1944, the county changed its name from former Zhongbu County to Yellow-tomb County, in honor of the Emperor.

The Yellow Emperor is believed to have been the leader of the alliance of all tribes in Chinese early society. According to legend, he invented many of China's notable accomplishments such as knowledge of the raising of silkworms, the construction of boats and carts, a system of writing, and the medical arts. For this reason he has long received the love and commemoration of the people.

His tomb is on the northern part of the county seat, on a hill called Qiao Mountain. It is 3.6 meters high, and it has a circumference of around 48 meters. Ancient trees grace the top of the hill and the scenery is lovely. Behind the tomb stands a stele with four large characters that was erected during the Qing dynasty and that commemorates the emperor. To the south of the tomb is a broad terrace, on which to make offerings to the great ancestor.

On the ridge of Qiao Mountain is also a Yellow Emperor Temple, which is also used for offerings and homage. Inside the grounds are ancient bo-trees, some of which may be upwards of one thousand years old. Among them is one tree that stands 19 meters high and whose branches are some ten meters long. Legends say that it was planted by the hand of the emperor himself. Before the great hall of the Temple are around 70 stelae recording the offerings made by dynasty after dynasty of emperors and kings who came to make offerings. In the center of the Great Hall entryway hangs a plaque extolling the Yellow Emperor as the creator of writing and therefore the earliest ancestor to lead Chinese into a civilized age.

People who come to pay respects at this temple can perhaps begin to understand the significance of this ancient person to the Chinese. He brought blessings upon the people through his outstanding achievements.

Ancient cypresses in the Yellow Emperor Tomb.

The Xuanyuan Temple commemorating Yellow Emperor.

Maoling Museum

◆ Address: Shaanxi Province, Xingping County
◆ Website: http://mlbwg.8u8.com

Maoling is located in Xingping County of Shaanxi Province, and is the tomb of the Han Emperor Wu Di (also known as Liu Che). Construction of the tomb was begun in 139 BC, and the tomb has been declared a National Important Cultural Protected Site. The Maoling Museum includes the tomb and exhibition halls of relevant cultural artifacts and architecture. It covers some 50,000 square meters with a building area of 7,600 square meters. The style of the building copies that of contemporary Han-dynasty houses.

A gold-plating copper horse of the Western Han dynasty displayed in the Maoling Museum.

The Maoling Museum currently has two exhibition halls. The eastern exhibits rare objects recovered from the Yangxin Tomb; the western has a permanent exhibit showing the historical artifacts of Western Han. TheWestern Han artifacts in both halls total 320 pieces, all of them excavated from within the precinct of the protected area around the Maoling Tomb. Very rare objects constitute around one third of the total.

The carved stelae and sculptures of this tomb are

one of its main attractions. These were done at the time and accompanied the burial of the emperor. Their artistry rivals such other well known Western-Han pieces as the Horse Trampling the Xiongnu sculpture: they occupy a significant place in the art history of world sculpture.

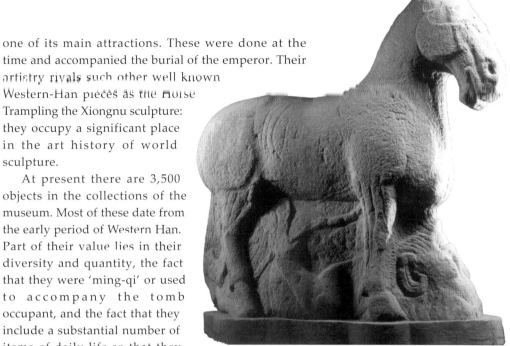

At present there are 3,500 objects in the collections of the museum. Most of these date from the early period of Western Han. Part of their value lies in their diversity and quantity, the fact that they were 'ming-qi' or used to accompany the tomb occupant, and the fact that they include a substantial number of items of daily life so that they help reveal the life and customs of the region at that time. The Maoling objects were executed with a high degree of craftsmanship and have the special Western-Han quality of being vital and confident.

The stone carving 'Horse trampling the Xiongnu' in front of the Huo Qubing's Tomb.

114

Qianling Museum

◆ Address: Shaanxi Province, Qian County
◆ Website: http://www.chnmuseum.com/js/sxql.htm

The Qianling Tomb is where the third Tang-dynasty emperor and his empress were buried together. The third emperor was Li Zhi and his empress was Empress Wu Zetian. This is the most representative among the eighteen Tang-dynasty tombs and the best preserved. It is located on top of Liangshan (Liang Mountain), six kilometers north of Qian County City in Shaanxi Province, around eighty kilometers from Xi'an. The scope of the tomb is very large with the precincts of the tomb and gardens totalling an area of 2,400,000 square meters.

Stone human statues outside the Qianling Tomb.

On the grounds of the Qianling Tomb, what one mainly sees today are extremely beautiful stone carvings that stand on top of the hill. They are arrayed in a line leading from the 'crimson sparrow gate' to the north and mark the 'way of horses and grooms,' the double line of statues leading up to the tombs.

The first pair of stone carvings are symbolic and indicate that this is a tomb; then come a pair of war steeds and crimson swallows. The steeds have cloud-pattern curling on their haunches, as though they were flying amidst the clouds. The crimson sparrow is depicted using high relief, with strong, beautiful carving. According to legends at the time, this mythical bird was sent as a funeral gift to commemorate the emperor from the king of what is now Afghanistan. It carried the symbolic meanings of both homage and protection, and so was carved into the stone before the tomb.

The stone carving 'Winged horse' standing in front of the Qianling Tomb.

Next come five pairs of stone horses, on which are carved saddles, stirrups and other equine accouterments. Originally each pair had stone grooms leading them but now only three remain. Behind the horses are ten pairs of retainers waiting on the emperor. They wear tall crowns and have broad-sleeved long robes that are belted at the waist. Their hands hold daggers and they look forbidding as they guard the tomb.

Two rows of stone stelae come next, with one on the right that is blank: it holds no characters or writing. This was put up on the orders of Empress Wu Zetian just before she died. She noted that her merit surpassed what later people could judge, and so they were not to write anything on the stele. It stands 6.3 meters high, and 2.1 meters wide, 1.49 meters in depth. Another stele, in contrast, holds some 8,000 characters, all of which were inlaid in gold after being carved so that their message could shine out over the empire. The text extols the civilized rule and military power of Emperor Gao Zong.

The tablet of 'No words' for Wu Zetian's Qianling Tomb.

A mural painting in the tomb of Princess Yongtai in the Qianling Tomb.

Behind the stone tablets on the right side of the horses and grooms way is a row of sixty-one stone statues of men. Almost all of their heads have long since been destroyed, but two remain to show us what they once looked like: these men had high noses, deep-set eyes, and were clearly people of Central Asia.

Two stone lions standing before the crimson swallow gate represent the finest works of sculpture at the Qianling Tomb. These are very large and ferocious: with curling fur, protruding eyes, open mouth and sharp teeth, they exhibit all the authority and power of the Tang dynasty.

According to historical documents, a number of accompanying tombs surrounded the Qianling imperial-tomb precinct. These were mostly robbed in antiquity but certain superlative works of art remain that can be seen at this museum. It is well worth a visit.

Dingling Museum

◆ Address: Beijing, Changping County, Special Area of the 13 Tombs
◆ Website: http://www.chnmuseum.com/dl1.htm

The Dingling Museum is located in Changping County at the foot of the Yanshan Mountains, outside Beijing. This is the site of the world-famous Ming-dynasty 'Thirteen Tombs' and it counts as the tenth among those thirteen. The thirteenth emperor of the Ming dynasty is buried here, together with his two empresses. Zhu Xianjun was the Shenzong emperor, with the reign

Overlooking the Dingling Tomb.

The portrait of the Ming Emperor Shen Zong – Zhu Yijun – who was buried in the Dingling Tomb.

name of Wanli. He ascended the throne at the age of ten, in 1572, and was on the throne for 48 years. This was the longest reign of any Ming-dynasty emperor.

The Dingling tomb construction was begun in 1584 and was finished in 1590. The cost of construction was said to be eight million liang of gold; it stands on 18 hectares of land. The main buildings are built along an axis that includes a stone bridge, stelae tower, gates, halls, tower, surrounding wall and the underground palace hall. The surface buildings were destroyed several times by fire, so except for the *minglou*, *baoding*, wall, and underground palace which have been relatively well preserved, only traces remain of the other buildings.

In May of 1956, archaeologists found the entryway to the underground palace at a depth of 27 meters. This was called the 'gold steel wall' gate and it stands 8.8 meters high. In it was a doorway shaped like the Chinese character for man. This entryway was tightly sealed with twenty-three layers of large bricks. Tearing down this human-shaped entryway in the gold steel wall, they followed along the corridor inside and encountered two large carved-jade doors. These were three meters high, and each of the two swinging doors in the frame was 1.8 meters wide and weighed around four tons. On them were carved nine rows of the symbolic knobs. A bronze beam of around ten tons in weight was set across the top part of the door: the axles of the doors were set in this so that they could swing open. Beyond the doors was an underground palace hall containing a suite of connected rooms, including front, middle, rear, left and right

A dragon robe unearthed from the Dingling Tomb.

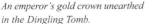

*An emperor's gold crown unearthed
in the Dingling Tomb.*

*An empress's phoenix crown unearthed
in the Dingling Tomb.*

chambers. All were spacious and separated by seven stone gates. The front and middle halls used 'gold bricks' as a floor covering, the others were of stone construction.

The rear chamber was the main part of the palace. Three coffins lay here, with Zhu Xianjun in the middle and his two empresses on either side. Twenty-six red-lacquered cases were set around the coffin, holding some 3,000 items made of gold, silver, gems, ceramics, jades, and fabric, all to accompany the burial.

All of the Dingling Museum's collections come from articles unearthed from this underground palace. They are not only beautiful, they represent a valuable resource for studying Ming court life and Ming craftsmanship.

Among items excavated from Dingling are the emperor's crown and a phoenix crown that are particularly notable. The golden crown is woven of very thin threads of gold and two golden dragons are crouched and coiled on top. The crown is 24 centimeters high with a diameter of 20.5 centimeters and a weight of 826 grams. The phoenix crown was used by the empress when she received visitors at court. It uses lacquered bamboo and silk as a base and on top are silk gold dragons and a jadeite phoenix, as well as flowers that are created out of gems. The crown is encrusted with 150 precious gems and more than 5,000 pearls.

120

Qing Dongling at Zunhua and Qing Xiling at Yixian

◆ Address: Zunhua Qing Dongling – Hebei Province, Zunhua County, Malan Yu

      Yixian Qing Xiling – Hebei Province, Yi County, Yongning Shan

The Eastern Tombs, or Dongling, of the Qing dynasty are located in Zunhua County in Hebei Province. They rest in the Malan Valley of the Changrui Mountains, some 125 kilometers from Beijing. The fifteen tombs located here include those of certain Qing emperors who reigned from 1644 onwards, including the tomb of the great Kangxi emperor. The tomb of the famous Cixi Dowager Empress is also located here. The fifteen tomb-mounds represent the largest and most complete grouping of imperial tombs that still exist in China today. They are arrayed east and west along the southern-facing slope of the southern ridge of the Changrui Mountains. The central axis of each tomb faces northward, towards a backdrop of mountains. The site is extremely beautiful, with ancient pines and long spirit ways gracing the approach to the royal resting places.

The heart of the Eastern Tombs is the tomb of Emperor Shunzhi, called Xiaoling. A total of five emperors, fifteen empresses, and 136 concubines are buried at the Eastern Tombs and all of these with one exception are arrayed to the east and west of this centrally located Xiaoling. The tomb of Kangxi is situated to the east and slightly south of Xiaoling. It was begun in the 20th year of Kangxi's long sixty-year reign (1681) and its size and scope are second only to Xiaoling. The tomb of Qianlong is set to the west of Xiaoling in the Shengxui Valley. It is a joint burial of the emperor, his two empresses, and three concubines. It too is a very special underground palace, with three rooms and four entryway gates; it reaches a depth of 54 meters and occupies 327 square meters of space. One notable aspect of this tomb is that all of its walls and ceilings are completely covered with stone carvings

The Qing Eastern Tombs in Malanyu in Zunhua County, Hebei Province.

relating to Buddhism. Several tens of thousands of characters of Buddhist scriptures also adorn the tomb, written in the clear and fluid lines of Sanscript and Tibetan scripts.

The tomb of Empress Dowager Cixi contains the most accomplished above ground artistry of all the Qing-dynasty tombs. It includes refined and exquisite stone carving that depicts phoenixes and dragons cavorting amongst clouds. The splendor of the architecture is unique, with gold foil fixed to the ceiling, superb painting, and fine carpentry of the actual structures. The tomb-chamber of Cixi has already been 'opened' and is the only tomb of an express's underground palace that has been excavated to date.

Four of the Qing-dynasty imperial tombs are located some 120 kilometers to the west of Beijing, in Hebei Province. These are known as Xiling or Western Tombs. This is where Emperor Yongzheng selected a site and began to erect his resting place. Eventually the location came to include the burials of three empresses, four emperors, and a number of princes, altogether 76 people in fourteen tomb groupings. Above-ground extant buildings occupy 50,000 square meters.

The organization of Xiling or Western Tombs is similar to the Eastern. Yongzheng's tomb, called Tailing, sits in the middle. The others are arrayed to his east and west. The spirit way leading up to Tailing is five li in length, or nearly two miles, and sculptures on either side are impressive. In the neighboring area twenty-one of Yongzheng's concubines are buried, also his empress, the blood mother of Qianlong.

To the west of the Tailing tomb of Yongzheng are two imperial groupings, one of which belongs to Emperor Daoguang. This includes buildings that are unique for not being painted but rather carved in dragon designs from nanmu wood. The dragons cover every inch of space on the ceiling, and the pillars and beams are alive with swimming dragons, coiled dragons, vigorous dragons.

To the east of Tailing is the most recent tomb among the western-tomb groupings, which was built for Guangxu and his empress. It is called Chongling. Groundbreaking began in the first year of Xuanzong (1909) and the work was completed in the fourth year of Minguo (1915). This was the last imperial tomb among all of China's imperial tombs and it holds Guangxu and his empress. This was robbed in early years, but when restoration and research of the site began in 1980 some jades and pieces of silk were found. Near the Chongling tomb are the tombs of various concubines.

All of these tombs have been declared National Key Cultural Relics Protected sites, and are listed also as World Heritage Cultural Sites.

The Qing Western Tombs in Yi County, Hebei Province.

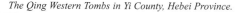

Hua-xia Civilization

    China is a large country with an ancient and well-developed civilization. Cultural aspects of Huaxia, such as silk, tea, ceramics, and Chinese medicine, have all made great contributions to mankind. Note that the term 'Hua-Xia' is broader in meaning than 'China.' It indicates more of a cultural space than a geographic designation, and also implies a historical lineage. 'Xia' is the name of the first-known dynasty of what later came to be 'China,' dating to some three millennia ago. The term 'Hua' includes both overseas Chinese as well as non-ethnic Chinese under the overarching umbrella of China.

China Silk Museum

◆ Address: Zhejiang Province, Hangzhou City, Yuhuang Shan, Northern Ridge

The external appearance of the China Silk Museum.

The China Silk Museum is in Hangzhou, on a hill called Jade-Spring Mountain that lies at the southern end of the lake. Including the grounds, the Museum covers an area of 73 mou and the building space covers 12,000 square meters. The complex of buildings is somewhat fan-shaped, or curved like a bow. A statue of the legendary god of silkworms stands in front. The 6,100 square meters of exhibition space inside the Museum are divided into the Silk Culture Hall, the People's Customs Hall, the Silkworm and Mulberry Hall, the Silk Manufacture Hall, the Silkweaving Hall, the Printing and Dying Hall, and the Modern Accomplishments Hall.

The first thing that greets the visitor in the entry hall to the museum is a large model of a Song-dynasty loom. Around its base is reproduced a Song-dynasty painting that depicts mulberry raising and silk weaving. The original of this painting is more than five meters long and was done by a court artist for the emperor. Through linked-painting technique, it systematically portrays the entire process of making silk, from planting mulberries and raising silkworms to unraveling the silk from cocoons and weaving cloth.

The Silk Culture Hall exhibits a large number of ancient silk artifacts, as well as models and photographs. Articles from the neolithic period include certain

items from more than 4,700 years and even a dyed piece
of silk woven fabric from more than 5,600 years ago.
Woven silk pieces excavated from the Jiangling Mashan
Chu Tomb in Hubei Province show the high level of
weaving technology during the Warring States period.

By the Han period, the development of Chinese silk
weaving had reached its first peak. The fabric excavated
from the #1 Tomb at Mawangdui that is exhibited here is
extraordinary. It lay underground for more than 2,000
years and yet is still as lustrous and beautiful today as it
was when it was buried.

During the Tang dynasty, silk weaving entered a
period of innovation due to extensive east-west cultural
exchange. The pieces excavated from a group of tombs at
Astana in Turfan, Xinjiang, exhibit the artistic style of
those times. Printing-on-silk technology was highly

*A pair of silk skirt-style trousers
of the Song dynasty.*

An ancient jacquard silk weaving machine.

developed during the Tang period. All of the printing technology methods that we have today were already in existence at the time of the Tang dynasty and some of these are exhibited here.

Woven silk fabrics in the Song and Yuan dynasties include numerous weaving techniques that are both complex and very beautiful. Weaving with gold came to be one of the more refined techniques and some pieces are displayed that were excavated from a site in Inner Mongolia. Silk brocades were used in the Song and Yuan periods but were most vibrant in the Ming and Qing dynasties. Exhibited here are a number of brocade items that were worn by emperors, empresses, and senior officials.

The Silkworms and Mulberry Hall exhibits the entire process of cultivating silkworms. On display are materials about some live mulberry trees in China that are over one thousand years old. The life cycle of a silkworm is shown, and specimens from around the country are on display. One can watch the birth and growth of the little worm, the way it spits out the silk and creates its own cocoon and the way that cocoon is then unwound to create silk threads. The Silk Production Hall gives the history of the tools of the trade. The Weaving Hall displays all kinds of traditional looms and allows visitors to actually sit at a loom and try for themselves. The Dying Hall has specimens of many kinds of plants and minerals that were used in traditional dyes. Nearby is also a small botanical garden that raises some of the plants used for these dyes. In addition to displaying the processes of dying, printing and embroidery, demonstrations are given by masters on the spot of the various techniques.

China Tea Museum

◆ Address: Zhejiang Province, Hangzhou City, Longjing Road, Double-peak Village

The China Tea Museum is at Xihu Lake in Hangzhou. It is composed of four separate buildings, each with a separate form and function. The first, a two-story building, contains exhibition halls and its sole function is to put on exhibitions.

This building displays the history of tea, and includes sections on tea implements and tea customs. The Tea History Hall begins with a section on Lu Yu (733-804), a Tang-dynasty figure who is revered as a tea saint and who excelled in the Way of Tea. A chronology of tea then systematically gives the development of tea in China, from Yunnan trees, to seeds, to development of the industry. A following hall displays all kinds of tea-processing methods that result in green tea, black tea, white tea, flower tea, pressed tea, Ulong tea and so on. These are accompanied by photographs

The exterior of China Tea Museum's Exhibition Hall

A wood carving statue of the ancient tea sage – Lu Yu – displayed in the China Tea Museum.

from tea-growing regions of China.

The Tea Affairs Hall introduces the planting, plucking, processing, preserving, and steeping of tea – all the various technologies that have to do with tea. The exhibition shows historic processing as done in the Tang and Song dynasties, but also has photographs of modern tea-factories and has modern tea processing factory models. In this hall are also modern methods of testing, connoisseurship about tea waters, and so on. The concluding portion of this hall displays photographs and information that describes the beneficial health effects of tea.

On the second floor are the Tea Implements Hall and the Tea Customs Hall. The treasures of the museum are located here. Some two hundred exquisite objects are displayed that were used as tea implements from early times to now. They include bowls, trays, bottles, kettles, cups, and so on. Song-dynasty ceramics include various famous glazes of the period, Ming-dynasty and Qing-dynasty pieces include imperial examples from the Palace Museum. Some items on display are from Japan, and there are a number of tea objects from Korea. One particularly noteworthy object is a large tea kettle used during the Minguo period. It stands some seventy centimeters high and has a diameter of around fifty centimeters and is an example of kettles that were in common use in Minguo tea houses.

The Tea Customs Hall shows scenes from five main tea-drinking regions of China. It reveals the variety of customs that have grown up around the culture of tea. Tibetan tea-drinking is shown here, for example, with a full set of implements and tea-related objects. A traditional scholar's tea-making arrangements are displayed. From Jiangnan or southern China, the Han people's tea-drinking customs are shown. From Yunnan, a bamboo pavilion is recreated that shows bamboo-segment tea containers and other tea-drinking customs of people in Xishuangbanna. There are also examples of gong-fu tea from Chaozhou, covered-bowl tea from Sichuan and so on.

The third building in the Tea Museum, which is set off by itself, contains five rooms with different and appropriate décor for serving different kinds of tea. The visitor can enjoy Japanese tea in a Japanese tearoom, Yunnan tea in a bamboo pavilion, Ming-dynasty tea in a Ming-dynasty teahouse. Guests are welcome to enjoy the variety and pleasures of tea.

Jingdezhen Ceramic History Museum

◆ Address: Jiangxi Province, Jingdezhen City, Xishi District, Fengshushan Fengjing Qu
◆ Website: http://www.travel-jx.com/jdz/bwg.htm

This museum is located in the Panlong Mountains, outside the city of Jingdezhen in Jiangxi Province. Panlong means 'curling dragons,' and the location of the museum is an ancient site for ceramic production in China that used the mountainsides for what are known as dragon kilns. The museum was built in 1980.

The earliest ceramics at Jingdezhen trace their history back more than 1,700 years, but the height of the fame and technology of Jingdezhen kilns came during the reigns of Kangxi, Yongzheng, and Qianlong in the Qing dynasty.

In addition to continuing the traditions of earlier successful glazes and techniques, many new forms of ceramic technology were

Egg-shell china.

An ancient porcelain kiln.

The blue-and-white porcelain.

invented here. Some are celebrated overseas, although few foreigners know their source. All of these are on display at the museum. The architecture of the Museum is in Ming and Qing style: buildings include display halls, workshops, glazing areas, stores, residences, a library, administrative areas, and other structures.

A porcelain statue.

The 'Qing garden' is one group of buildings within the museum area. It lies in a secluded and quiet forested valley. It copies a famous Qing-dynasty structure called the Yuhua Tang, with traditional construction and carving. The décor is simple and elegant, and the building contains some ancient stone horses as well as some of the ceramics described below. What attracts most attention at this Jingdezhen Ceramics History Museum are the exhibits of valuable ancient ceramics and the demonstrations of handicrafts by which these ceramics were originally made.

In the great hall of the Yuhua Tang some of these valuable ceramics are on display. They include recently excavated examples of Ming-dynasty pieces from the reigns of Yongle and Xuande. The glazes are lustrous and soft, the pieces are dated with reign marks and are masterpieces of the art at the time, with tremendous artistic as well as scientific research value.

In neighboring simple and unadorned handicrafts workshops, craftsmen use ancient implements to demonstrate traditional arts. Focusing single mindedly on making beautiful replicas, they demonstrate the entire process of creating ceramics. More than 150 older artisans, together with a younger generation that is carrying on the tradition, can be seen kneading clay, fashioning vessels, applying underglazes. The production process is basically the same as was recorded in Ming and Qing period histories. The workshops are themselves works of art, for they are replicas of the ancient ceramics craftsmen's actual architecture. The entire presentation represents the most complete set of handicrafts systems that has been come down to us from the Qing dynasty.

'Hu Qing Yu House,' Chinese-Medicine Museum

◆ Address: Zhejiang Province, Hangzhou City, Dajing Xiang, #95
◆ Website: http://www.huqingyutang.com

At #95 Dajing Xiang in Hangzhou is one of the rare remaining commercial establishments from the late Qing period that is in its original condition. This is the famous southern-Chinese medicine house of Hu Qing Yu. Today, this house has been restored and made into China's first Chinese pharmacopoeia museum.

It is said that the predecessor to Hu Qing Yu was a medicaments maker in the southern Song dynasty. By the time of the Tongzhi 13th year of the Qing dynasty (1874), an Anhui businessman named Hu Xueyan built the national brandname of Hu Qing Yu on this foundation, and in the process started China's most famous pharmacy.

Stepping over the simple doorjamb and through an austere door, one passes through a corridor on which hang many illustrations of fables and tales that relate to the medicaments of the house. On the opposite wall are hung more than thirty brand names of famous medicines. Once

The medicine house of Hu Qing Yu.

one reaches the great hall of the actual enterprise, a gold-lacquered wooden high counter is always one's first impression. Behind it is a cabinet 'of a hundred eyes,' holding many small drawers which hold as many potent remedies.

A long corridor full of boards that introduce all kinds of medicine.

The rear room of the enterprise was used by what were called counter-watchers, the accountants who tallied up the actual transactions. This was the main place for selling the goods. Today it has become the Hu Qing Yu Chinese Medicine Museum exhibition hall. All kinds of ancient implements and artifacts used in the conduct of the herbal medicine business are on display here. Further back in the building is where the medicine was made. Herds of deer were once kept behind the house, that were used in the making of the medicine known as Melliuu Lu. Before a deer was killed, a sign would be hung out to advertise this fact and to attract people to come watch, in order to prove that Hu Qing Yu used only authentic materials in its 'Deer Pills.'

Traditional pharmaceutical tools collected by the medicine house of Hu Qing Yu – a gold shovel and a silver pan.

Hu Qing Yu's ancient architecture not only has historical and artistic value, but it is also interesting in terms of the history of the business. It is said that Hu Xueyan did some calculations and figured out that building this establishment would cost him 200,000 taels of silver. He reckoned that each year he would expend 2,000 taels, but still the income brought in by just having this building would far outweigh the cost of any other

134

The inscribed board that reads "No cheating" inscribed by the shop owner hung in the shop.

The interior gate of the business hall of the medicine house of Hu Qing Yu.

method of advertising. This was Hu Xueyan's rationale for building a quite expensive and handsome building. Anyone who came to his store would become a mouthpiece to advertise his wares: they would all take on the duty of promoting Hu Qing Yu. The logic seems to have worked.

Quanzhou Overseas-relations History Museum

◆ Address: Fujian Province, Quanzhou City, in the tourist cultural district of East Lake
◆ Website: http://travel.qz.fj.cn/fengguang/haijiaoguan.htm

The new Quanzhou Overseas-relations History Museum was built in 1990 on the eastern shore of the lake. It has three exhibition halls: 'Quanzhou and ancient overseas relations,' 'Quanzhou religious stone sculpture,' and

The exterior of the Quanzhou Overseas-relations History Museum.

The model of a restored sea boat of the Song dynasty unearthed in Quanzhou.

复造古船复原模型
THE RESTORED MODEL OF THE ANCIENT
SEA FROM WU-ZHU

A sea boat of the Song dynasty unearthed in Houzhugang in Citong, Fujian.

'Quanzhou export ceramics.' There is also a 'Quanzhou Bay Ancient Ship Exhibit' located in the old Kaiyuan temple. Together, the two locations of the museum cover 35,000 square meters, and the exhibition space approaches 4,000 square meters.

The Quanzhou Bay Ancient Ships Exhibit is located on the east side of the Kaiyuan Temple. A total space of 1,307 square meters is divided into the reception hall, the ships hall, and a hall for artifacts that have been excavated from ocean-going vessels. The reception room has the aspect of a harbor. The ancient remains of a ship that is 24.2 meters long and 9.15 meters wide are exhibited here and constitute one of the most important of the exhibits.

Items excavated from oceangoing vessels are displayed on the second floor. Exhibited are things from shipwrecked ocean vessels that have been recovered, including a Song dynasty ship that was excavated in 1982 – the objects that accompanied that Fashi ship are displayed here as well as a 1 to 10 model of the ship itself.

The Quanzhou and ancient overseas-relations exhibition hall are located in a

A tablet display of Arabic denizens who lived in Quanzhou in the Song and Yuan dynasties.

Quanzhou Chinawares sold for abroad of the Song and Yuan dynasties – 'junchi.'

space that is divided into chronological dynastic sections. These display the circumstances surrounding Quanzhou's ancient commerce. The exhibition includes 200 photographs and 300 objects.

The Quanzhou religious sculptures are located in the east exhibition hall. Around 300 sculptures are on display that were left in Quanzhou and passed on to later generations by religious representatives of the Song and Yuan periods. Religions represented include, most importantly, Islam, also Nestorian Christian and various religions from India.

The Quanzhou Exhibition of Export Ceramics is on the second floor of the exhibition hall. According to a set timetable, exhibitions rotate from neolithic period to modern Quanzhou-area ceramic production, as well as a comprehensive exhibit of ceramics through all periods. Some 420 antique ceramic pieces are included, as well as a small number of new pieces. In addition to the three special exhibits that are open to the public, on the second floor the Quanzhou Overseas-relations History Museum has an 800-square meter space in which is exhibited 'China's Customs History.' This is organized with the cooperation of the Customs General Administration, and with the Customs service of Xiamen and the Customs service of Quanzhou.

The Quanzhou Overseas-relations History Museum has a total of 3,000 objects in its collections. Among these, several dozen are first and second-grade cultural relics. Of these, the ancient articles excavated from ancient ships and the religious sculptures are considered most valuable. Among the collections of this museum are also some that relate to the history of overseas Chinese, and there are also Spanish silver coins and such foreign articles from the time when Quanzhou's overseas-relations were at their height.

Assembly of Talents:
Arts and Literature

China has made outstanding contributions to the world in more than just the material realm. It has also made contributions in the area of spiritual civilization: it is an ancient Eastern country with a highly refined human culture. The following institutions highlight different aspects of this culture.

China Fine Arts Gallery

◆ Address: Beijing City, Dongcheng District, May 4ᵗʰ street, #1
◆ Website: http://www.ccnt.com.cn/visualart/mcprc/under/meishu/mcprc715.htm

The China Fine Arts Gallery is located on May-Fourth Road in Beijing (Wusi Dajie). It is a national-level art museum that concentrates on works by China's modern painters. The Museum covers a total area of 30,000 square meters, with a building area covering 17,051 square meters and an exhibition space of 6,000 square meters. The Museum has three levels and 13 exhibition halls: recently rebuilt and expanded, the new museum is quite handsome.

The China Fine Arts Gallery collects, conserves, displays, and researches superlative artworks of modern Chinese artists and also folk art. It organizes a variety of Sino-foreign exhibitions, supports academic exchange and research, and publishes collected works as well as essays on art theory. It has more than 60,000

The corridor and courtyard of the China Fine Arts Gallery.

The exhibition hall of the China Fine Arts Gallery.

The facade of the China Fine Arts Gallery.

objects in its collections that encompass modern and contemporary art and people's folk art. Some ancient paintings are also held in the collection, as well as some works of art from other countries.

As a cultural focal point open to both Chinese and foreigners, the Gallery often puts on many types of exhibitions. Other than the permanent exhibitions organized by the museum itself and jointly sponsored exhibits from other museums, it also holds short-term exhibits that explore brave new initiatives and give exposure to different Chinese regions. In order to heighten international communication in the arts arena, the Gallery often holds exhibitions brought in from other countries. The collections of the Fine Arts Gallery have also been abroad on exhibition many times. Every year, the Gallery holds more than 100 exhibitions in Beijing, and every year it receives several million visitors.

Since its founding, the Fine Arts Gallery has held around 60 large-scale national exhibitions that display the collections of the museum itself. Since the 1980s, more than 100 exhibitions have been held of works from abroad, such as the French 19th-century Village Views Painting Exhibition, the Boston Museum of Fine Arts Famous American Painters' Original Works Exhibition, the Rodin Art Exhibit, the Famous Painters of Western Painting Exhibit, as well as many art exhibits with Australia, Japan, Russia, Germany, Korea, Malaysia, Norway and Israel.

Selected works of the China Fine Arts Gallery have visited France, America, Japan, Russia, the Czech Republic, Turkey, Greece, and Korea, and have travelled many times to Hong Kong, Macao, and Taiwan.

The Oil Painting Portrait of Qi Baishi *painted by Wu Zuoren.*

China Modern Literature Museum

◆ Address: Beijing City, Chaoyang District, Shaoyao Ju, Wenxue Guan Road, #45
◆ Website: http://www.wxg.org.cn

The China Modern Literature Museum is located in the Chaoyang District of Beijing. The Museum constitutes the primary resource in China for materials on Chinese modern literature and it is also the largest building in the world dedicated solely to literature and to collections relating to literature. Resources include a library, a documents hall, a hall for research materials, and a

The exterior of the China Modern Literature Museum.

The statue of Bing Xin displayed in gardens of the China Modern Literature Museum.

A portrait of Ba Jin collected by the China Modern Literature Museum.

center for academic exchange. The mission of the museum is to collect, conserve, organize, and research works of modern and contemporary authors of China, their manuscripts, translations, books and letters, diaries, recordings, videos, photographs, documents and any other materials that relate to the critique of a work such as literary journals and newspaper reviews.

The China Modern Literature Museum was established in March of 1985. Its collecting principles do not distinguish on the basis of political views, artistic school or sect or style. All new literary materials since the beginning of the 20th century can be collected, including works from Hong Kong, Macao and Taiwan, and also overseas Chinese-language works. The museum currently has more than 300,000 collected items, among them 170,000 books, 2,100 kinds and 90,000 copies of magazines, 142 kinds of newspapers, 10,970 handwritten manuscripts, 8,282 photographs, 7,887 letters, 453 taped recordings, 773 videos, and 2,959 cultural artifacts.

The Museum has set up special rooms or cases for whole collections that have been donated to the museum. It has also set up collections in the name of the person donating. Such cases include the special collections of Ba Jin (1901-), Bing Xin (1900-1999), Xia Yan (1900-1995) and some fifty more authors, including those from Hong Kong, Taiwan and overseas such as Lin Haiyin (1918-2001), and Bu Shaofu (1909-2000).

The China Modern Literature Museum actively carries on all kinds of literary activities, and has collectively edited a number of works on modern authors, as well as editing a quarterly journal together with the Modern Literature Research Association. Scholars both in China and abroad have carried on

The garden in the China Modern Literature Museum.

extensive interaction through the work of this museum. They have organized some major exhibits such as a retrospective of the works of Lao She (1899-1966) of Ye Shengtao (1894-1988), and an one-hundred-year tribute to Mao Dun (1896-1981).

The Museum has a multi-capacity hall that is offered for use as a site for literary discussions, research, speeches, performances, and exhibitions. A television hall is set up for televised events, and there is a media production room. The Museum is in a secluded garden full of trees. Inside, certain works of art were created specifically for the new museum by famous sculptors, painters, and craftsmen. There are oil paintings on the walls, colored glass inlaid in the walls, authors' sculptures, authors' signatures on ceramic vases and so on, providing an artistic atmosphere that is comfortable and conducive to reflection.

Beijing Theater Museum

◆ Address: Beijing, Xuanwu District, Hufang Road, #3
◆ Website: http://www.bjmuseumnet.org/museum/xiqu/one.htmlChina

Among the hundreds of halls built during the Ming and Qing dynasties, the one called Huguang Huiguan is best preserved of them all. It was originally built in 1807, in the twelfth year of the Jiaqing reign of the Qing dynasty. It is situated at the southwest corner of the intersection at Hufang Qiao. In 1997, it was completely renovated and reopened as what is now called the 'Beijing Theater Museum.'

The most valuable part of the complex is a theater building that was constructed in 1830. This is the most ancient of all of China's extant indoor theaters. The floor space of the first floor measures 568 square meters and the second floor is 328 meters, making a total of 896 square meters for the theater. The stage is 54 square meters. The main structural elements are the two great beams and nine crossbeams that span 11.36 meters, which is rare among buildings in China.

Today, eight-sided tables are placed around the lower level, and upstairs are boxes for seating; altogether the theater can hold an audience of 250. The ancient theater has been repainted but has not lost its refined elegance.

The old Xiangxianci building is currently the exhibition hall of the theater museum. It gives a brief history of the development of theater and in the process one can see that the institution of such a *huiguan* or gathering spot was very important for the development of Peking opera. In the Qing dynasty, when theaters from elsewhere came into Beijing they used the *huiguan* theaters for performances. The Anhui Huiguan would perform Hui-plays, the Huguang Huiguan would perform Chu-plays, the Jiangxi Huiguan would perform Gan-plays: this allowed all the different kinds of theater the opportunity to see each other and draw inspiration and lessons from each other. The exchange and blending finally created the conditions for the birth of the ultimate Chinese theater, Peking opera. Some of the masterpieces of the theater were first performed in the Anhui Huiguan, such as Peach blossom Fan. Great masters of the stage such as Master Tan Xinpei (1848-1943), Mei Lanfang (1894-1961) and others have all in the past performed here. Historical treasures relating to the theater are stored in the Xiangxianci part of the Wenchang pavilion. There are, for instance, the costumes worn by Yang Xiaolou (1879-1938), there are early period records made by the EMI Company, and so on.

147

The main gate of the Beijing Theater Museum set up in Huguang Guildhall.

148

China Sports Museum

◆ Address: Beijing City, Anding Men Wai, Anding Road, #3A
◆ Website: http://www.bjkp.gov.cn/kpcg/kpcg/bowuguan/newpage225.htm

The China Sports Museum is located in Beijing on the southeast side of the Olympic Center outside Anding Men. The building is quite extraordinary. It opens out like an octagonal fan, or like a whirlwind that is about to take off, symbolizing the powerful development of Chinese sports.

The China Sports Museum is the first specialized museum devoted to collecting, exhibiting, and researching sports culture and sports-culture history. It covers 7,100 square meters, including an exhibition area of 2,510 square meters. It holds seven exhibition halls altogether, that exhibit five main types of objects. A large stone-carved statue of a dragon boat greets the visitor in the main foyer. Dragon-boat

The exterior of the China Sports Museum.

The Song dynasty One Hundred Play *carved on stones.*

racing is the quintessential traditional Chinese sport and therefore this fine, inlaid version of a dragon boat is appropriate.

The first hall holds the ancient Chinese sports section. This has a strong ethnic flavor: dragons coil up the golden pillars, palace lanterns are hung high above, everything feels ancient. The exhibition moves chronologically from pre-Qin, to Han and Three Kingdoms, Westerm and Easterm Jin, North and South dynasties, then Sui, Tang and Five dynasties, Song, Liao, Jin, Yuan, Ming and Qing. All reflect the accomplishments of China's ancient sports development. Items displayed include photographs, pictures, rubbings, documents and historical material, and such archaeological works as the Tang dynasty polo players.

The second hall is for China's modern sports from 1840 up to the year 1949, explaining the changes in this period through the use of historical photographs and actual objects. For example, the earliest China football team cards, dating from 1902, are displayed; there is a special edition of a 1904 sports magazine, photographs of China's participation in the first Far East Sports Rally, the 1936 Berlin Olympics, and so on.

The third, fourth and fifth halls exhibit the sports accomplishments of the People's Republic of China. Using more than 500 objects and more than 500 photographs, this portrays the support of the party and the government for sports enterprises. It includes competitive sports as well as general recreation sports, and covers sports arena design, sports psychology, and so on, all of these reflecting the past forty years of Chinese sports accomplishments. The sixth hall uses more than 300 photographs and around 500 objects to display special qualities of China's various regions and 56 national minorities. It portrays local traditional sports in particular.

After visiting this museum, Samaranchi, the former Chairman of the International Olympic Committee noted that, 'The China Sports Museum is one of the best sports museums I have seen in the world.'

Hong Kong Museum Of History

◆ Address: Hong Kong Special Administrative Region, Kowloon, Tsimshatsui, Chatham Road South, #100

◆ Website: http://hk.history.museum

The Hong Kong Museum of History was formerly called the Hong Kong Museum. The new museum was opened to the public in 1998; it is located in Tsimshatsui, Kowloon. The permanent exhibition of this museum shows 'The Story of Hong Kong,' which portrays in a lively way the natural ecology, local customs, historical developments and traditional culture.

The Museum currently has over 45,000 objects in its collections, which are

The Hong Kong Museum of History.

divided into archaeological, local history, people's history, and natural history. Among the archaeological objects are items discovered on China's southeastern shore, and articles excavated in the 1930s in the southern islands.

Archival photographs are an important historical resource and the Museum collection is rich in these, with the earliest dating back to the 1860s. Other objects in the collection include models of town and village architecture, early newspapers and documents, a complete set of Hong Kong money, and family genealogies from an old town in the New Territories.

Collections relating to people's customs include fishing equipment and models of fishing ships, traditional clothes, village furniture and daily articles, items relating to local customs and beliefs, dolls, entertainment items and so on. The natural history collections include shells of sea animals, butterflies, and all kinds of gems and minerals.

The Hong Kong Museum of History has held more than 60 thematic exhibitions since its establishment, such as Fifty years of Hong Kong archaeology, Living history: protecting the historical architecture of Hong Kong, Hong Kong money, Hong Kong historical materials, Hong Kong postage stamps over 150 years, and so on. These

An old gramophone collected by the Hong Kong Museum of History.

A corner of the interior display of the Hong Kong Museum of History – models of Fujian sea boat and painted trade boat.

The night scene of Hong Kong.

An ancient style street scene in Hong Kong.

exhibitions have wide-ranging subject matter. They go deeply into Hong Kong history from various perspectives, and they have been helpful in enhancing cultural exchange between Hong Kong and neighboring regions.

Macao Maritime Museum

◆ Address: Macao, Mage Street, Mage Temple Qiandi #1
◆ Website: http://www.museumaritimo.gov.mo

The Macao Maritime Museum is located near the Mage Temple on Mage Street in Macao. It was established and opened to the public in 1990 and is a specialized museum focusing on maritime relations. It is under the jurisdiction of the Macao Port Office.

The Maritime Museum "was built for the mariners' friends of all the world's peoples." The building is a completely enclosed construction of three levels. It is located on the

The underground exhibition area – maritime folk custom.

southwest end of the Macao peninsula, next to the harbour. Nearby is the #1 wharf where a Huating and a dragon boat are docked, which are also for visitors' enjoyment.

The Museum currently has around 2,000 objects in its collection. These introduce the boats in which Portuguese came to Macao in the early period, as well as traditional Chinese ships and equipment. Included are also navigation tools used in Macao today. Exhibitions are divided into the fishing industry, Portuguese and Chinese discoveries, technology, and transport.

The fishing section introduces fishing equipment and fish-cultivation

The exterior of the Macao Maritime Museum.

The exhibition area in the 2nd floor – Maritime history.

The exhibition area in the 3rd floor – Navigation technology.

technology. Models of boats, nets, ways to catch fish and some scenes of fishermen actually catching fish are shown. The section on Portuguese and Chinese discoveries shows how the Portuguese Vasco da Gama led a fleet to this area in the late 15th century, how he discovered the passage to India and how other Portuguese explorers came to the Malaysian archipelago and on to China and Japan. The early period of China's maritime industry is also described, with the history of Zheng He heading out on the western seas in the early 15th century.

The Museum also exhibits a large number of military weapons and devices used on the high seas, such as guns, cannons, telescopes and so on, showing the importance of the defense of trade routes.

Gardens and Architectural Monuments

China has long been renowned as a birthplace of gardens. The grounds and buildings of ancient Far Eastern gardens are masterpieces of the art of merging man and nature in a harmonious whole. They also unify art and technology.

Suzhou Gardens Museum

◆ Address: Jiangsu Province, Suizhou City, Jingde Road, #274

◆ Website: http://www.szgarden.sz.js.cn

Suzhou is known as a Garden City. As the saying goes, 'The gardens south of the river are first under heaven, while those of Suzhou are the crowning achievement of those south of the river.' These exquisite gardens are the ultimate expression of China's ancient architecture and arts, and they are the distillation of the cultural history of the famous city of Suzhou.

The marvelous quality of Suzhou's gardens lies in the fact that they use a tiny amount of land to realize the creative abilities of the craftsman. The twists and turns allow a new view at every step and allow the revelation of microcosms of gardens within gardens and macrocosms of views outside of views. When you walk into a garden you suddenly put yourself in a painting. Among the many gardens, four have been declared the masterpieces: these are the Canglang Pavilion of the Song dynasty, the Lion Forest of the Yuan dynasty, the Zhuozheng Garden of the Ming dynasty, and the Liu Yuan of the Qing dynasty. These represent the artistic styles of their respective dynasties.

The Lion Forest.

In order to commemorate the 2,500th anniversary year of Suzhou, a Gardens Museum was established inside the Zhuozheng Garden. Its buildings use the former residential structures of the garden. The southern part of the museum adjoins Northeast Street; the north is connected to the flower gardens of the Zhuozheng Garden. The whole covers 1,696 square meters, with an architectural space of 1,350 square meters. The exhibitions in this museum mainly introduce the history of Suzhou's ancient gardens, plus their current conditions and the technology of building gardens. There are four exhibition halls.

The first describes the objective reasons for basing such superlative gardens in Suzhou: the preconditions, including mountains and rivers, the ancient history, the flourishing economy, the confluence of peoples and the many generations of skilled artisans.

The second describes the history of the gardens. This gives a comprehensive overview of their development and progress. The gardens began in the Spring and Autumn periods of the Zhou dynasty, long before China was unified in 221 BC. By the time of the Wei, Jin and the North and South dynasties, temples and private families were creating different kinds of gardens. In the Song and Yuan dynasties, piled up rocks became the rage, in the Ming and Qing eras garden pavilions flourished.

The third hall introduces the contours and styles of Suzhou's ancient gardens as they are today, as well as the international influence of these gardens.

The fourth introduces garden construction. This reflects the many-layered approach of Suzhou's gardens, the layering of mountains, water, buildings, flowers, trees. All are blended together to form the four great traits of a garden. Traditional artistic constraints are used to create both poetic meaning and visual results.

The main displays in this museum are models that show arrangements of gardens, especially those that no longer exist. There are twenty-four such displays, including Suzhou-style gardens built abroad and other famous gardens of the South. Zhuozheng Garden is an example of gardens within the museum; it uses miniature mountains and rock crags to create its illusions. A number of other gardens use water as their main component. Both the gardens themselves and the museum are well worth visiting.

Zhuozheng Garden.

The Lingering Garden in Suzhou.

The Summer Palace

◆ Address: Beijing City, Haidian District, Xinjian Gongmen Road, #19
◆ Website: http://www.yiheyuan.com

The Summer Palace, located in the western suburbs of Beijing, is the last imperial garden built by the feudal dynasties of ancient China. It was destroyed by the British and French Allied Armies in 1860; the Empress Dowager Cixi (1835-1908) then appropriated the navy's budget to rebuild it. In 1998, this imperial garden, which belongs to world civilization, was entered in the ranks of World Cultural Heritage.

Entering the garden from the East Palace gate, one first passes through an impressive gate and comes upon seven halls that are situated facing eastward. These are the 'Morally Upright' halls where

The Yulan Hall in the Summer Palace where Emperor Guangxu read and called in subordinates.

the Qing emperors met with various ministers. Inside are preserved the thrones used by the Empress Dowager and the last Emperor Guangxu while they were on the throne. Also on display are various paraphernalia of the time including incense burners of bronze dragon and phoenix, candlesticks, the mythical beast called the 'chilin', and the screen that is so pervasive a part of Chinese culture.

Passing further westward, one soon comes to the lake, and to a hall, Yulan

Wax statues of 'An eunuch combing hair for Cixi' displayed in the Summer Pavilion.

Tang, that was built for the relaxation of the Emperor Qianlong. This was rebuilt in the 18th year of Guangxu and made into a sleeping chamber for the Guangxu Emperor. In 1898, after Cixi put the Reform Movement into motion, she locked Guangxu up inside this small palace. She had the corridors to east, west and north all sealed or blocked up with brick walls, while the southern entryway was watched day and night by a eunuch that she personally trusted.

The Leshou Tang Main Hall was the resting palace of Cixi. To the left and right on the stairs are around six different kinds of bronze

The famous Long Corridor along the Kunming Lake.

deer, cranes, and vases, that signify peaceful togetherness. The suite to the west was Cixi's bedroom. The rooms to the east were for changing clothes. Subsidiary halls to east and west were stations for female officials and palace women who were on duty.

On the northern bank of the Kunming Lake is a long corridor, also called the thousand-steps corridor, that is world-famous for its fine craftsmanship. It contains 273 small 'rooms' and is 728 meters in length—the longest corridor in any form of Chinese garden or ancient architecture. The four octagonal pavilions that are spaced along it, for stopping and resting, have ornate descriptive names and symbolize the four seasons. Some 8,000 paintings are painted directly on the beams of the corridor. They narrate stories of famous people in Chinese history and portray decorative scenes.

The Buddhist Incense Pavilion.

The central axis of the entire garden is formed by drawing an imaginary line from the central ridge of the backdrop of the Wanshou Mountain, from to the Buddhist Incense Pavilion. A hall called the Parting the Clouds Hall graces the mountain ridge and is considered the most beautiful of the entire garden. It can be reached by ascending a set of stairs and will reward the visitor with lovely sights. To the north of the hall stands the south-

The Marble Boat.

The night scene of Suzhou Street.

The big stage in Dehe Garden.

central ridge of the Wanshou Mountain, and on that stands the central building of the Summer Palace, the Buddha Incense pavilion. Three Buddha statues are inside the Pavilion, which stands an impressive 41 meters tall.

In the western end of the long corridor, beside the lake, is the only structure in the Summer Palace that has a western character. This is a stone boat that is 36 meters long. The cabin on it is made of wood, and it is furnished with western-style tables and chairs. A number of other locations in the Summer Palace are of both historical and aesthetic interest, with the so-called Eight Views of Hui Mountain being among them. When the Qianlong Emperor took his famous southern tour, he viewed an ancient garden in the town of Wuxi and resolved to build a replica of it on his return to the north. This became the Huishan Bajing, the Eight Views of Huishan at the Summer Palace.

The Summer Palace was invaded and destroyed first by the English and French Allied Army and then again by the Eight-Powers United Army. It underwent extensive restoration and was reopened in various stages, starting in 1986. In 1992, other buildings were reconstructed on their original sites; in 2003 Qianlong's garden plans were basically restored. This outstanding Chinese Imperial Garden Museum is famous worldwide not only for its construction and views but also for its rich collection of art. More than 4,000 items are in the collection, among which some 300 are regarded as extremely rare treasures.

164

China's Great Wall Museum

◆ Address: Beijing, Yanqing County, Badaling
◆ Webpage: http://www.bjmuseumnet.org/museum/chchg/one.htm

The majestic appearance of the Beijing Badaling Great Wall.

Coming to China and not visiting the Great Wall is like going to Egypt and neglecting the pyramids. It is the equivalent of not really visiting the ancient civilization. One of the architectural wonders of the world, the scope of the Great Wall dates from when the Qin dynasty unified China. It reaches a hypothetical 'ten thousand *li*' from east to west: its name in Chinese literally means the ten-thousand-*li* Long Wall. This term is descriptive: a *li* is roughly one-third of a mile and ten-thousand li signifies a very long distance. Different parts of the Wall were constructed through the many dynasties of Chinese history, over the course of more than two thousand years. In extent, though not in one connected line, the different parts of the Wall stretch from the portal known as Jiayuguan in Gansu in the west all the way to the pass called Shanhaiguan in Hebei in the east. During the Ming dynasty many parts of the wall were rebuilt using stone blocks and earthen bricks that had been used before. The resulting Wall represents much of what can be seen today.

The Great Wall in the vicinity of Beijing's

'Badaling Pass' is the best part of the Ming-dynasty reconstructed wall. This section uses stones as the foundation and pounded-earth as the core, and is faced with a special kind of brick. Its average height is 7.8 meters and average breadth is 6.5 meters: it could accommodate five or six horses riding abreast along the top. At intervals along the wall are towers for both surveillance and for shooting; also fire towers that were used to transmit military information. Portals allow passage at certain intervals: the great portal outside Beijing is known as Juyongguan.

In 1994, a 'China's Great Wall Museum' was built on the western side of the Badaling Pass. Its exhibition hall covers 3,000 square meters and is divided into several exhibition rooms. The permanent exhibition is composed of eight

The autumn scene of the Beijing Badaling Great Wall.

The Jiayu Pass in Gansu Province.

The tablet erected when the Huangyaguan Great Wall was built in the Ming dynasty.

different parts: the historical Great Wall, the Ming-dynasty Great Wall, the building and fortifications, the Great Wall's military and political significance, economic and cultural exchange along the Great Wall, literature and arts, Love My China Repair My Great Wall, the First among Famous Places, and Rainbow of Friendship. Exhibitions in these various sections display all kinds of historical objects and show functions of the Wall that included both peaceful economic exchange and protective military power.

In addition to the locations for viewing the Great Wall north of Beijing, many other parts of the Wall can be visited as well. The portal in the far west, called Jiayuguan, is known as the 'greatest pass under heaven' and is well worth visiting. The one in the east, at Shanhaiguan or 'Mountain-Ocean-Pass,' is of tremendous significance in Chinese history. All of these are open to visitors and have historical objects on display.

The Mutianyu Great Wall.

Temple of Heaven

◆ Address: Beijing, Chongwen District, Tiantan Road
◆ Webpage: http://www.jsdj.com/luyou/lyzy/Bjtiantan.htm

The Temple of Heaven is located in the southeastern part of modern-day Beijing, on the east side of Yongdingmennei Street. It once lay outside the ancient city precinct and was the site of imperial offerings to heaven during the Ming and Qing dynasties. Over the course of thousands of years of imperial offerings in China, it is the only one of such sites remaining today. A group of buildings, gardens, and surrounding groves, it is highly symbolic and is a museum of a very special nature. The State Council has declared it to be a key cultural protected unit and in 1998 it was listed by UNESCO as a World Cultural Heritage Site.

A heaven sacrificing and harvest praying ritual performance held in the Qinian Hall in the Temple of Heaven.

The Yuanqiu Altar in the Temple of Heaven in Beijing.

The Imperial Vault of Heaven in the Temple of Heaven.

Construction of the Temple of Heaven was begun in 1420, during the Ming dynasty under the Emperor Yongle. After Yongle had settled on Beijing as the site of the capital, the buildings and surrounding areas were later rebuilt and enlarged during the reigns of Jiaqing and Qianlong of the Qing dynasty.

The general layout of the Temple of Heaven incorporates the ancient Chinese configuration of a 'round heaven and a square earth.' This symbolic form ties in to a north-south geographic alignment, with the concept of 'north-round-south-square.' Two layers of walls surround the temple precincts. The outer wall's circumference is 6,553 meters with a space inside of 270,000 square meters, which is about four times the size of Beijing's Palace Museum. The site once occupied a large percentage of what was the outskirts of ancient Beijing.

The Qigu Altar and the Qinian Hall

These two are located in the northern part of the Tiantan complex. They comprise a large and imposing set of buildings and are the most representative architecture of the Temple of Heaven. The lower part of the Qinian Hall is a three-tiered white marble round platform, surrounded by a stone railing. The upper part is a round-shaped hall that is built without cross beams. Its ceiling is arched and pointed and its roof is covered with blue glazed tiles. The circumference of the lower tier of the platform is 90.8 meters and its total height is 5.56 meters. The Hall is located in its very center, and has a diameter of 32.72 meters and a height of 38 meters. The top part of the Hall holds a round-shaped baoding or topknot that is gilded. Twenty-eight cypress (nanmu) pillars are arrayed around the Hall. Inside the hall, stand four dragon-well pillars with diameter of 1.2 meters, and height of 19.2 meters. The ambiance of this hall is enhanced by the way the ceiling rises towards the sky. On the northern side inside the hall is a dragon-carved throne on a supporting dais, and a stele to the ancestors and gods of the emperors. On a special day of the first month of every year, the emperor would lead his princes and officials here to pray for good harvests, and, if they were encountering drought, they would come here to pray for rain.

On the various sides of the Qinian Hall are subsidiary buildings that were used for various imperial purposes. Altogether they form a harmonious group.

The Yuanqiu Altar and Imperial Vault of Heaven

This altar is not as grand as the Qinian Hall but is still a very important part of the Tiantan, for this is where the emperor made sacrifices to heaven. The altar was built in the 9th year of Jiaqing, or 1530. It was originally covered in blue-glazed tiles. In the 14th year of Qianlong (1749) it was expanded and was faced with marble, taking on its current aspect. The altar is round and divided into three levels, each with nine stairs leading up it on each of the four cardinal directions. In the center of the top level is a round central stone, with nine circles of stones arrayed around it. Each level has numerous indicators of nine or of multiples of nine. The craftsmen took pains to emphasize this number, since it was seen as an indicator of 'yang' or the male principle, and this in turn was seen as a confirmation of the intent of heaven.

Behind the circular altar lie a group of buildings including a round structure called the Emperor's mystic realm or Vault of Heaven. These buildings were begun in the 9th year of Jiaqing (1631). They were repaired in the 8th year of Qianlong (1743). They include a circular hall with pointed roofline, inside which the ceiling extends upward in layers. A carved stone base holds a stelae that celebrates the emperor. The thing that most attracts people's attention at this place is the 'echo' wall that surrounds it as well as the so-called triple-sound stones.

In addition to the temples and altars comprising the main architecture of the Tiantan, a number of subsidiary buildings exist that were used for operational purposes. These included rooms for cooking, preparing the sacrifices, and storing things. A building called the Zhaigong is where the emperor would sleep before making the sacrifices and praying to the gods of harvest. Another site of interest is believed to be one of the earliest groups of buildings at the Tiantan. It was built in the 18th year of Ming-dynasty Yongle (1420), and was specifically made for music to accompany the sacrifices. It served as a practice room for the music masters, and was also used for storing the instruments. From this, we can understand how important music was as an integral part of the imperial rites.

The Confucius Temple, Family Seat, and Woods

◆ Address: Shandong Province, Qufu City
◆ Website: http://www.cnwh.org/cnsites/nsk/kmklkf.htm

Qufu, in Shandong Province, was the capital of the ancient State of Lu,
dating back some 3,000 years ago. It is regarded as one of the famous

*Confucius sacrificing ritual performance held in the
Dacheng Hall in the Confucius Temple in Qufu.*

historical cities in Chinese history, and it is also the homeland of the late Spring and Autumn-period philosopher and educator known as Confucius. In Chinese, this man is known as Kongzi; he was a historical person who lived from 551 to 479 BC. The passage of history has layered Qufu with many cultural traces – among the most notable of these are the Confucius Temple, family seat, and woods, which occupy the smaller half of the town.

Confucius Temple

The entryway to this temple passes through a precinct that is dotted with ancient trees and that leads the visitor through a passageway of cypresses. The entry is from the south, through the southern gate of the ancient town. A forest of stone stelae testifies to the long history of the place, which measures some 327 *mu* in size and is more than one kilometer in length from north to south.

The main building of the Confucius Temple is called the Dacheng Hall. It is a magnificent building enhanced with 28 coiled dragon pillars and vermilion and golden tiles. Successive generations conducted rituals here in honor of Confucius. Rituals began in the second year after Confucius died, namely in 478 BC, when Lu Aigong turned Confucius' home into a temple. Since that time, dynasty after dynasty of emperors have remodeled and renovated the place, till it has arrived at its current state. The buildings of the temple copy the layout and style of imperial palaces, with nine courtyards and a central axis that runs north-south. There are some 466 rooms in the Confucius temple, with numerous halls and pavilions, in addition to 55 gate buildings.

The dragon pillars of the Dacheng Hall in the Confucius Temple.

The Family Seat

To the east of the Confucius Temple is the family seat. It has been the site of official offices as well as the private home of many generations of the Sage. It covers an area of more than 240 *mu* and includes 463 halls and rooms. It has nine courtyards divided by three passageways: the eastern passageway is where the family shrine is located. The western passageway contains the study of the Sage, where he read books and studied poetry and the rites.

The main part of the family seat is located along the middle passageway. Before this are situated a number of palace administrative offices. The rear part is the residence, and at the very rear is the garden, which is called 'Iron Mountain Garden.' A large number of works of art are preserved in the family seat, the most famous of which are ten Shang and Zhou-dynasty bronze vessels for offerings. With their elegant forms, exquisite ornamentation, and clear inscriptions, these are considered some of China's rarest treasures. One of the fine paintings in the collection is of the Three Sages by the Yuan-dynasty painter and calligrapher Zhao Mengfu. A copy of a portion of the *Confucian Analects* is on display that is written in such small script that one can read it only by using a magnifying glass. Even more valuable are the nearly ten thousand scrolls and documents from the Ming and Qing

The main gate of the Confucius Residence – the Lingxing Gate.

The residence of Kong Lingyi – the 76ᵗʰ generation of Confucius.

dynasties. From many different perspectives, these reflect the political, economic, philosophical and cultural aspects of ancient China.

Woods

One arrives at the famed Confucius woods after leaving Qufu by exiting through the northern gate and passing through the row of cypress trees and exquisitely carved stone stelae. The woods occupy 3,000 *mu* of land and are where Confucius and his descendants are buried. This area represents the best-preserved and most complete set of ancestral clan tombs in China. Going through the Sage Woods Gate, one arrives at an arboretum that was planted, tree by tree, by the many generations of disciples of Confucius.

The Confucius Tomb in Confucius Woods.

Jin Ancestral Hall Museum

◆ Address: Shanxi Province, Taiyuan City, Nanjiao District, Jinci Town
◆ Website: http://www.sxta.com.cn/lvjd/tyjc.htm

The Jin Ancestral Hall is located in Taiyuan City of Shanxi Province, 25 kilometers to the south of the city, at the foot of a mountain. This is the oldest architectural monument remaining in China that has confirmable historical documentation. It also has the oldest garden, and is hallowed ground that melds natural scenery with an ancient human presence.

The Jin Ancestral Hall is located at the source of the Jin River. It was constructed in the Tang dynasty, at the imperial ceremonies surrounding the confirmation of Shu Yu. It was officially dedicated to the King of Zhou, Zhou Chengwang, who lived in the eleventh century BC. Because of its location on the Jin River, Shu Yu changed the name of the kingdom to Jin, and in paying respects to Shu Yu life, later generations named the place the Jin Ancestral Hall. Although the buildings have been renovated and expanded many times, the original site has not changed. In the years 1023-1032, during the Northern Song dynasty, an additional Sacred Mother Temple was built and the Ancestral Hall was substantially enlarged. In 1168, during the Jin dynasty, another commemorative hall and other buildings were added, until it gradually came to assume the shape and size that it is today.

An iron man of the Song dynasty in the Jin Ancestral Hall Museum.

The Naolaoquan Pavilion in the Jin Ancestral Hall Museum.

The flying beam bridge in the Jin Ancestral Hall Museum.

The Jin Ancestral Hall Museum includes the original buildings of the place, the gardens, and woods, the spring, the sculpture, and the carved stelae. Key items on exhibit include, most importantly, the Sacred Mother Temple. This is one of the earliest remaining large-scale wooden buildings in the world, with unique spatial arrangement, internal structure, and artistic form. There are 43 Northern Song-period painted statues inside the hall, treasures among painted clay sculpture in China. The main statue is of the Sacred Mother, who sits in a wooden case in the middle of the Hall. The other 42 are arrayed on either side as well as around the perimeter of the Hall.

A great flying beam bridge is set across the square-shaped fish pond in front of the Sacred Mother Hall. This bridge was built in the Tiansheng period of the Northern Song and is built in the shape of a cross. It sits on 34 small octagonal stone pillars that are set in the water on stone-carved lotus blossoms. A *dougong* construction is set on the pillars, with traditional-Chinese crossbeams and blocks. On these are set the beams and the planks of the bridge. The surface of the bridge is covered with bricks, and stone railings line on either side. On the moon platform on the eastern side of the bridge is a pair of iron lions that were cast in the 8th year of Zhenghe, or in 1118.

Another of the great treasures in this place is an inscribed stele erected in the Guan Bao Han Pavilion. This stands 195 cm in height, is 127cm wide and 27cm

Lady-maid statues of the Song dynasty in the Shengmu Hall in the Jin Ancestral Hall Museum.

thick, and holds an inscription that was written by the Tang emperor, Tang Taizong. It is composed of 203 characters and is written in cursive script.

The spring that is the source of the Jin River is the primary reason the Ancestral Hall is located in this place. This spring is clear and pure and runs year-round at a constant temperature of 17 degrees centigrade. It waters a number of trees in the vicinity, one of which is an ancient cypress that is said to be 3,000 years old. The flow rate of the spring is 1.8 cubic meters per second: this emerges from a pavilion that stands over the actual source, and then is channeled into north and south canals.

The ancient buildings of the Ancestral Hall also hold a collection of valuable artifacts. In addition to the Hall, other ancient architectural monuments include an Ancestral Hall to Shu Yu, a water-reflecting pavilion, a golden-man platform, a clock and drum tower, and a sacred long-life temple. A library also enriches the substantial holdings of this ancient place.

Homes of Our Fore-bears: Archaeology

The vast lands of the cultural continuum that has come to be called China are one of the cradles of early man. From Paleolithic to Neolithic periods, early people have left their advancing footprints on this land.

Beijing Man Site Museum

◆ Address: Beijing City, Fangshan District, Zhoukoudian Xiang

◆ Website: http://www.cnwh.org/cnsites/nbjr/zkd.htm

The site of this historic archaeological discovery, set on a low hill called Dragon-Bone Mountain at Zhoukoudian, 50 kilometers to the southwest of Beijing, marks one of the origins of early man. The resulting finds became known to the world as 'Peking Man' or Beijing Man. Because of this, the site was declared an important National Cultural Protected Unit in 1961, and was listed as one of UNESCO's World Cultural Heritage Sites in 1987.

Autumn is the most congenial season in Beijing, and is also best at Dragon-

The exterior of the Beijing Man Site Museum.

Bone Mountain. The reconstructed dioramas at the exhibition hall of early man that describe a period some 400-500,000 years ago are also set in the fall. Beijing Man utilized the southward migration of deer and other animals to surround and hunt these tasty wild creatures. Women and children plucked ripe berries and fruit in this season, and also gathered grains in preparation for the cold winter.

The site of Zhoukoudian is set into a mountainside, with running water available nearby. Natural caves existed in these mountains and the weather was warmer long ago. The natural environment was conducive to habitation and Beijing Man is believed to have lived here continuously for some 300,000 years. Evidence of this habitation has been left behind in the caves, in the forms of bones, worked stones, and traces of occupation.

The main cave measures 140 meters from east to west and 53 meters from north to south. At twilight on a cold early winter's evening in 1929, with the help of a lighted candle, archaeologists crawled into the space of this cave and found the extraordinary discovery of a complete early hominid cranium from 500,000 years ago. The name given to it was China Primitive Man, Beijing-type. Or, in short, Beijing Man.

Beijing Man left several tens of thousands of Paleolithic stone tools behind him in this and neighboring caves, made in many shapes and from many types of stone. These can be seen in the exhibition cases of the museum. Through long periods of experimentation, Beijing Man became familiar with the different uses and chipping qualities of different kinds of stone. Beijing Man's use of fire deserves special mention: these people were in possession of the knowledge of how use fire to cook food, stay warm, give light, and keep off wild animals. The use of fire delineated an epoch-making chapter in the history of man's advancement.

The restored head statue of the 'Beijing Man.'

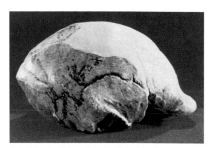

The Beijing Man Crania found in the Beijing Man Site in Zhoukoudian.

The restored image of Beijing Men going hunting.

In 1973, the so-called 'New Cave Man' was discovered at Zhoukoudian, representing a stage in man's history of advancement to 'early hominids,' dating to 200,000 to 100,000 years ago. Around 20,000 years ago, the humans living in the vicinity of Zhoukoudian were given the name Mountaintop Cave Man following their discovery in a cave above the Beijing Man Cave. This earlier discovery was made in 1933, and indicated that the inhabitants had already entered a matrilineal-clan commune stage. The most representative works of the Mountaintop Cave Man were an 82-millimeter bone needle, its surface still shiny and slightly arced in shape, with one side still very sharp. On the other end some very fine instrument had hollowed out a tiny hole. The appearance of this object proved that the Mountaintop Cave Man already sewed and clothed himself with animal hides and leather. A number of interesting ornaments were excavated from the site, including earrings, animal teeth with holes in them for stringing, fishbones, ocean shells, stone beads, bones carved in certain ways, and so on. This indicated that people of the time had an appreciation of aesthetics and of how to adorn themselves.

Xinle Site Museum

◆ Address: Liaoning Province, Shenyang City, Huanggu District
◆ Website: http://www.chnmuseum.com/xl/1.htm

The Xinle Site Museum is located in the northern part of the Huanggu District of Shenyang City, Liaoning Province. It is divided into northern and southern components: the southern has an exhibition hall for displaying cultural relics, while the northern is the actual archaeological site and is an important protected cultural property. The northern section covers an area of 22,500 square meters and preserves a large-scale primitive dwelling site by reproducing in open-air form ten dwellings from the Neolithic period, together with a simulated lifestyle of people living at that time.

The discovery of this Neolithic site was first made at the Xinle Electric Power Plant, hence the name. The excavations are divided into Upper Strata and Lower Strata cultures, with the Upper Strata belonging to a period roughly 3,000 years ago. This corresponds with the bronze period, and excavated objects include ceramics such as three-legged vessels and stone tools that are predominantly of the polished-tool type. The Lower Strata belongs to a period roughly 7,200 years ago, or what is considered to be a primitive-society Neolithic period. Half-submerged or half-underground dwellings reveal the contemporary architecture. Recovered artefacts include deep-bellied pots with impressed rope patterns, microliths, polished stone tools, chipped stone tools, carbonized particles, and wooden carved items. Since this culture had unique characteristics and was important in researching the history of early peoples in the northeast, it was given the name Xinle Culture.

After repeated excavations, the Xinle site has produced around thirty habitations in the Lower Strata Xinle Culture. Larger buildings are around 120 square meters in area, medium-sized are around 40-60 square meters, and small-sized are around 20-30 square meters. These are spaced closely together in lines so that this is considered to be a Neolithic settlement.

The Xinle Site Museum in the southern district currently has around 1,200 objects in its collection. In the northern district of the museum, one half-underground house has been preserved and is on view in its original state. This homesite was excavated in 1978. It is rectangular in shape, covers 95.46 square meters, and there is a round hearth in the middle. The four walls of the pit show the remaining traces of columns. A large number of items were excavated from within the house that are now exhibited mostly in the form in which archaeologists found them at the time. This, together with the actual structure of a dwelling that people used 7,000 years ago, gives visitors an authentic sense of what it was like to live here at that time.

The unique architectural external appearance of the Xinle Site Museum.

Hemudu Site Museum

◆ Address: Zhejiang Province, Yuyao City, Hemudu Town
◆ Webite: http://www.hemudusite.com/

The Hemudu Site Museum is located in Hemudu Town, Yuyao City, Zhejiang Province. The site dates from the early Neolithic period in southern China. It covers forty thousand square meters and has a cultural layer that is a total of 3.7 meters in depth. Four separate cultural layers can be distinguished that, after calibrated carbon fourteen testing, date to between 7,000 and 3,500 years ago. In 1982, this site was declared a National Key Cultural Protected Unit.

The Hemudu Site Museum was opened in May of 1993 and is divided into two parts: the actual site of excavation and an exhibition of objects. It covers a total of 26,000 square meters and the building area covers a space of 3,163 square meters. The building area is composed of six separate buildings that are joined to one another by corridors. The general layout of the buildings conforms to the unique Hemudu style of architecture, which in Chinese is called *ganlan*-style, or trunk and railing. This includes a long ridgepole, short eaves, and a high foundation. The building rests on 456 pillars on which lie groups of cross beams, symbolizing the tenon and mortise technology already used some 7000 years ago. The foyer is in the shape of a legendary 'roc' spreading its wings, expressing the worship of birds that was practiced by the early Hemudu

A bone spade-like plough unearthed in Hemudu.

The exterior of the Hemudu Site Museum.

people.

This museum exhibits around 3,000 objects that were retrieved in two main excavation periods at the site. Among the objects are remains of rice kernels planted by man, ceramic fragments that have traces of carbonized rice grains, rice-husk-patterned pottery fragments, bone items, wooden joint pieces, ivory bird-shaped artefacts, ivory carved plate-shaped containers with sun motifs, jade items, and so on. These are all worthy of being described as gems of neolithic culture.

The original state of the Hemudu Human Residence Site.

The exhibition is divided into two parts, the permanent exhibition and the specimens exhibition. The permanent exhibition has three halls. The first covers 400 square meters and explains the basic situation of the 7,000-year-old site in terms of charts and photographs. The second hall covers 300 square meters, and reflects the hunting and gathering life as well as the rice-agriculture of the time. It exhibits actual items such as man-cultivated grain, agricultural implements made of bone, a husker made of wood, and stone grinders, ceramic axes, etc., as well as containers for holding food, appropriate for an exhibition of rice-producing culture. The third hall covers 400 square meters and includes two parts, one on the life of the settlement and one on its spiritual or intellectual culture. Exhibited here are pillars, beams, boards and other wooden architectural elements, wooden tools, stone ax, stone awl, bone awl, a reconstructed trunk and railing style building (portion), and a model of a well. Parts of a primitive loom are also displayed, including many things that no longer have contemporary names.

The restored external appearance of the Hemudu Human Residence.

Banpo Museum in Xi'an

◆ Address: Shaanxi Province, Xi'an City, Banpo Road, #1

The exterior of the Banpo Museum in Xi'an.

The Banpo Museum is located in a modern building some three miles to the east of Xi'an City in Shaanxi Province. It is near the bridge that crosses the river, long renowned as one of the famous eight rivers of Chang'an. The Museum was built in 1958 and is the first museum built for a 'mankind site,' a habitation site of early man. Its name comes from its location on the northern side of Banpo Village. The site marks a settlement that dates to the matrilineal clan commune period of the Neolithic period. Before its discovery in the twentieth century, it had been lying in wait for some 6,000 years.

The arrangement of the Neolithic village was quite organized. At the center of the settlement was a 160-square meter-large room that was surrounded by many smaller rooms. All of the doors of these faced the inside larger room, reflecting the clan spirit of a cohesive group. Around the village was a 300-meter long trench or ditch that was used to keep wild animals from attacking. To the east was a ceramic-making area and to the north was the cemetery district. Inside the town were some 46 houses. Some were square, some round, some half-submerged in the ground, some on the surface. These houses already used traditional Chinese wall-construction methods and can be called precursors of later Chinese architecture that used wood and earth.

In a reconstruction of a Banpo room are exhibited production tools and daily utensils that were used by Banpo people. On the walls are hung animal skins and pointed-bottom vessels for getting water. A mat is spread beside the hearth on the floor – the scene of ancient man's life is suddenly spread before our eyes: members of the clan, under the direction of the old grandmother, are just in the process of

A basin of human face and fish pattern unearthed in Banpo.

A bottle with sharp-pointed bottom unearthed in Banpo.

Part of the Banpo Residence Site.

making a fire. Or outside, hunters are taking aim and firing their arrows or are vigorously throwing out flying balls, pursuing a frightened spotted deer. By the river, fishermen are in the process of catching fish, in the virgin forests, women and children, holding bone spades, are gathering wild fruits. As the sun goes down in the west, the village, sparkling with kitchen fires, shows women roasting meat, using stone grinders to grind meal, using bone needles to sew hemp-fabric clothes. Artists are focusing on painting or impressing patterns into ceramic vessels; old grandmothers are carefully distributing the cooked food to the others: some people are putting gathered vegetables and grains into vessels for storage.

In the northern part of the Banpo Village is the cemetery district where adults were buried. Some 174 graves have been discovered, lined up in regular order, but exhibiting different burial customs. Banpo people mostly died around the age of 30. On the eastern side of the town is the Public Kiln for firing pottery. Six kilns have been found to date. At the beginning, the pottery making was carried out in the open. By the time of Banpo, people had invented two main types of horizontal and upright kilns. Banpo ceramic production used both fine-grained clay and sandy coarse clay; the fine-grained was of three types depending on its use. Banpo people used realistic methods of painting to decorate their ceramics, with sketched designs to exhibit the characteristics of various animals.

Around twelve different kinds of markings or symbols have been found on pottery fragments or on vessels at the site. Together they comprise the main types of strokes used in Chinese characters, such as upright, cross-wise, hooked, and so on. Writing did not exist at the time, but these marks or symbols almost certainly contained their own meanings for people at the time. A number of daily articles are also exhibited in the museum, such as stone axes, finely made fishhooks, fish-bone forks, sharp bone needles, and all kinds of ornamentation made of stone, bone, and ivory.

Marvels of Heaven and Earth: Natural History

China's natural history museums express the common attempts of mankind to understand the world in which we find ourselves. The following describes a selection of museums that explore various aspects of our world.

190

Beijing Ancient Observatory

◆ Address: Beijing City, Dongcheng District, Jianguomen Dong Biaobei Hutong, #2

This museum looks like a turreted tower set in Beijing's ancient city walls. It is located on the southeast corner of Jianguomen Street in Beijing. When it was originally built, in the Guo Shoujing (1231-1316) period of the Yuan dynasty, it had a slightly different name but the same intent: to explore the heavens. Over the course of more than five hundred years, through Ming and Qing dynasties and on into the period after the Xinhai Revolution (1911), this location has been used to observe phenomena of the skies. This is the longest historical record of using any such observatory for so long. At present, eight large bronze implements

The Beijing Ancient Observatory.

Part of ancient astronomic apparatus displayed on the Beijing Ancient Observatory.

for viewing the heavens are arrayed on the top of the museum's tower; these date from the Qing dynasty. Under the tower is a hall built between the years 1442 and 1446, during the Ming dynasty. To the east and west are subsidiary rooms and other ancient structures.

The observatory's platform, rebuilt in recent years, is 17 meters high and holds exhibition rooms inside. If you walk through the door with the three characters for the observatory carved above it, you find a three-level exhibition space devoted to China's ancient astronomical accomplishments. A stone-carved star map from Suzhou is exhibited here, as well as the ceiling astronomical map from Longfu Temple, two rare treasures. The former was done in the Song dynasty in the year 1247. It depicts 1,434 stars and is recognized as one of the best early star maps in the world. The latter was accomplished in the Ming period, but from the characters carved on the side of the map one can see that the underlying information already existed in the Tang dynasty. In the courtyard of the museum, surrounded by ancient trees, the hall and east gate areas exhibit early astronomical instruments and the methods and changes in making them. In the western chamber some 150 early methods of calculating calendars in China are exhibited. Archaic as well as more recent astronomical water clocks and contemporary astronomical clocks are exhibited. Eight bronze astronomical instruments are arranged on the top of the platform, as per the Qing-dynasty emperor Qianlong's instructions.

Geological Museum of China

◆ Address: Beijing, Xisi, Yangrou Hutong, #15
◆ Website: http://www.bjmuseumnet.org/museum/dizhi/one.htm

The Geological Museum of China is located in Beijing at a place called Western Crossroads. It is an internationally renowned geological museum with the largest, rarest, and most valued collections in China. Its buildings cover some 11,000 square meters and contain around 200,000 items.

Begun in 1916, the museum is one of the oldest in China. In 2004, the rebuilt museum opened to the public, with an exhibition area of 4,500 square meters. It now has an earth sciences hall, an ore hall, a paleobotanical hall, a gems hall, and a land and resources hall.

The Museum's collections are extremely rich and contain many superlative Shantungosaurus giganteus fossils, rare fossilized primitive birds, the world's

The Geological Museum of China.

A pillar-shape quartz crystal cluster of orpiment.

A trilobite fossil.

largest quartz crystal (3.5 tons), the largest mono-crystal, and so on. The earliest hominid fossil to be found to date in China is exhibited here, known as the Yuanmou-Man tooth fossil from Yunnan Province. Artefacts from Zhoukoudian, the early-hominid site outside Bei-jing, are also on display here.

As well as presenting material for public view, the Museum has been a research organization that carries on projects and produces publications. In this regard it has made great contributions in several areas that include dinosaur research, volcanic-activity research, work on botanical bridging of plants in the Jurassic period, and work on primitive birds in western Liaoning through fossil research that has particularly received recognition from paleobotanists around the world.

194

Zigong Dinosaur Museum

◆ Address: Sichuan Province, Zigong City, Dashanpu

◆ Website: http://www.zdm.cn

The Zigong Dinosaur Museum is located in Dashanpu at Zigong City, on the banks of a river that flows through the western-China province of Sichuan. It is China's first museum located at the actual burial site of dinosaurs and it covers 25,000 square meters.

The exterior of the Zigong
Dinosaur Museum.

The exhibition hall that maintains the original state of excavating site of dinosaur fossils in Dashanpu, Zigong. *The exhibition hall of dinosaur fossils in Zigong.*

'Sichuan's dinosaurs are numerous and one finds a veritable nest of them at Zigong.' Zigong is a famous city for salt production, but it is also an important dinosaur fossil region in China. As a famous saying goes, one finds a veritable nest of dinosaurs at Zigong. There are more than forty locations within the city at which dinosaur fossils from different eras have been found. A very considerable amount of fossilized dinosaurs has been excavated here and other vertebrate fossils have been found as well at the same sites.

The concentration of buried fossil remains at Zigong is greatest at Dashanpu. A great quantity and diversity of types is found here, including specimens that are quite rare and relatively well preserved. This place is eleven kilometers to the northeast of Zigong City. It was discovered in 1972. The fossils are in a sandy layer of the Meso-Jurassic period, from around 160,000,000 years ago. In an area of around 3,000 square meters, more than 100 individual dinosaurs have been excavated, among which some thirty are complete or relatively complete dinosaur skeletons. Especially valuable is a group of dinosaur skulls. At present, only around twenty percent of excavated dinosaurs in the world belong to the Jurassic period, and most of these are from the late Jurassic, lacking the early and middle stages that show how dinosaurs evolved. At Zigong, especially at Dashanpu, the fossils come mostly from the early and middle periods, so that this provides extremely valuable material.

The newly built Zigong Dinosaur Museum mostly exhibits fossils of dinosaurs that have been excavated from the immediate site. The exhibition is divided into three parts:

Part 1 introduces general knowledge about fossils, botanical evolution, geologic periods, the evolution of dinosaurs and species extinctions.

Part 2 introduces the group of dinosaurs from Dashanpu. In a large space, viewers can see dinosaurs that stand 10 meters high and are 20 meters long, as well as tiny dinosaurs.

Part 3 is the actual site of dinosaur burials, in an exhibition area of 1000 square meters. This has dinosaur bones in their original setting. Observers can look down from a railing above, but can also go down into an underground room and touch the fossils of ancient life, see the circumstances of the layers and the ores, understand the wonders and marvels of the creations of nature.

Tonglushan Ancient Metallurgy Museum

◆ Address: Hubei Province, Huangshi City, Daye County, Tonglushan Town
◆ Website: http://www.chnmuseum.com/js/hbtle.htm

Tonglushan or Tonglu Mountain is 28 kilometers from the important heavy industry town of Huangshi in Hubei Province. It is on the banks of Daye Lake which connects via waterways to the Yangzi River. Archaeologists discovered several hundred mining pits in this location and a number of copper-ore smelting furnaces that date from the early period of Western Zhou (around 3,000 years ago) to the Han dynasty (around 2,000 years ago), or over a period of one thousand years. Tonglushan is considered to be the cradle of ancient bronze culture in China.

In the process of extracting ore resources from under Tonglu Mountain, it was discovered that this was a large-scale refining or smelting site from ancient times. Archaeologists have to date excavated and evaluated remains from Western Zhou to Western Han periods. They have found different mining structures and support systems for several hundred wells that include vertical wells, slanted wells, blind wells and so on, as well as more than one thousand implements for mining and ore production and various implements of

The copper mining tools of the Spring and Autumn period.

The crisscross mining lanes in the Ancient Copper Mine Site.

daily life. In addition, they discovered seventeen Song-dynasty smelting furnaces. On entering the front door of the Museum, one passes around a mammoth malachite boulder. The 1,100 square meter main hall of the site is then before one's eyes. Below the railing, looking down, one can see more than one hundred relatively well preserved vertical wells or shafts, level corridors or lanes, blind wells, slanted wells, criss-crossed mine tunnels. There are twisting channels for waterways and wooden water troughs, there are various implements of the trade spread below one's eyes. All of this makes one feel as if the workers in had just departed.

The exterior of the Tonglushan Ancient Metallurgy Museum.

In certain places, pits and corridors have been reconstructed to allow visitors to go inside and experience for a moment the sensations of those who worked here 2,000 years ago. On walls surrounding the main hall, traditional architectural techniques have reconstructed the original posts and brackets of the Spring and Autumn Period in Chinese history.

Due to the wealth of copper ore in this location, and the long history of refining ore here, the amount of waste ore from the process is noticeable. To this day, on the surface of the ground surrounding the ore lode, there are more than 400,000 tons of ancient remains of slag. It is estimated that this site produced 8-100,000 tons of copper. The quantity of materials at the site are testimony to the outstanding technology of refining and production methods of ancient China.

Most of the ancient wells or pits that have been excavated are situated in regions that are rich in natural copper, cuprite or red copper ore, and malachite. Since the copper content of some ore taken from the wells reaches 12-20%, it can be seen that ancient craftsmen possessed the ability to read indications of promising locations. In terms of prospecting, they did shallow well testing and used washing and other methods to find high-quality ore buried beneath the surface of the earth.

In terms of extraction, under non-mechanized conditions, craftsmen used the most simple tools and materials to dig wells that were more than fifty meters deep. They created effective ways to combine vertical, slanted and blind wells with horizontal corridors; they resolved to a certain degree the problems of supporting the wells, creating air ducts, allowing for light, and expelling water. Their solutions to complex technical issues were sometimes later found in use in Europe, therefore it was once believed that some techniques had been imported. From this archaeological research it is now clear that certain structural supports and technical solutions were in use in China 2,500 years ago.

In terms of refining, the distribution of the smelting slag is extensive: the thickness of the resulting slag layer approaches three meters so that it even buries abandoned refineries that once existed here. Because of this, the slag layer preserved the surface of the land in its original state, and kept this sole example of ancient mining technology intact.

Zigong Salt Industry History Museum

◆ Address: Sichuan Province, Zigong City, Ziliujing District, Jiefang Road, #107

The Zigong Salt Industry Historical Museum is situated in Zigong City, Sichuan Province. Its buildings utilize China's traditional architectural methods: an 86-meter-long central axis comprises the central hall, with the subsidiary group of buildings going up the slope of a hillside.

The exhibitions of this museum begin with an illustration from a Han-dynasty brick that was excavated in Sichuan. The illustrations on the brick depict the salt industry of the Han period and show in a lively and realistic manner the stages of salt production. Wide-mouthed shallow wells were used for early production; a two-story building and four men on the brick show how briny water was brought by conduits to heating units that cooked out the water and resulted in pure salt.

By the time of the Song dynasty, Chinese craftsmen had invented special tools for digging small-mouth-diameter wells. Not only was the mouth of the well sometimes 'as small as a small bowl' but it was dug

The picture shows the ancient salt production in China.

A wood well tower in traditional salt drilling wells in Zigong.

All kinds of drilling wells and dredging tools in ancient salt wells in China.

down very straight into the earth. The tools for allowing this well-tunnelling method are recorded in the 'Dongpo Forest of Stelae,' also exhibited at the Museum.

By the time of the transition period between Ming and Qing dynasties, the depth of these so-called Zhuotong wells reached three hundred *zhang*, a *zhang* being 3 1/3 meters, or around 1,000 feet. This museum has in its collections a relatively complete set of well-digging tools, that not only could dig deeply but ensured that the well's cavity would be straight. Some modern-day well-digging technologies are a result and a continuation of this historical foundation.

Joseph Needham (Cambridge University Professor, 1900-1995, Englishman, a world-famous historian of science and technology) listed more than twenty important inventions that had entered Europe from China in his 'History of Science and Technology in China.' The fifteenth of these was the deep-well drilling technology. It is on display and well worth seeing in this unusual museum.

The exterior of the Zigong Salt Industry Historical Museum

China's Museums Cultural China Series